LORAN LANDSCAPING
2344 WINNIPEG ST.
REGINA, SASK.   S4P 1H3
PH. 565-8855

 LORAN LANDSCAPING
Box 1458
LaRONGE, SASK.
S0J 1L0
PH: 425-3675

LORAN LANDSCAPING
841 2nd. AVE., S.E.
SALMON ARM, B.C.
V1E 4C7 833-4778

a guide to estimating landscape costs

a guide to estimating landscape costs

Edited by

Gary O. Robinette

and
the Staff of the
Center for Landscape Architectural Education and Research

VAN NOSTRAND REINHOLD COMPANY
New York

Van Nostrand Reinhold Company Inc.
115 Fifth Avenue
New York, New York 10003

Van Nostrand Reinhold Company Limited
Molly Millars Lane
Wokingham, Berkshire RG11 2PY, England

Van Nostrand Reinhold
480 La Trobe Street
Melbourne, Victoria 3000, Australia

Macmillan of Canada
Division of Canada Publishing Corporation
164 Commander Boulevard
Agincourt, Ontario M1S 3C7, Canada

16 15 14 13 12 11 10 9 8 7 6 5 4 3

Library of Congress Cataloging in Publication Data
Main entry under title:

A Guide to estimating landscape costs.

    Bibliography: p.

    1. Landscaping industry—Estimates. 2. Landscape
gardening—Estimates. I. Robinette, Gary O.
II. Center for Landscape Architectural Education and
Research.
SB472.565.G84   1983   712′.068′1   83-1048
ISBN 0-442-22343-9

a guide to estimating landscape costs

INTRODUCTION

This book is an attempt to gather information and material commonly used in estimating landscape costs into a form which becomes a ready reference to those persons needing such information. To gather and organize such material is an extremely difficult task for many reasons. Basically however, the problems of regionalism, inflation, different relationships to time and materials, as well as different methods of calculation of information present the greatest difficulties.

Regionally many different materials are used throughout the United States and Canada. Also within each of these regions a variety of different methods and techniques are utilized to handle material or to calculate labor costs. Any dollar figures that are assigned to any specific function, activity or material, of course, are obviously subject to inflation. Materials which were prepared in the 40's, 50's or 60's are totally out of date in the 70's or 80's. Therefore it is possible to give, as in this book, some information with the caveat or warning that a significant factor for inflation should be placed on any of these dollar figures. Obviously there are many different relationships as well as techniques and methods of calculation from office to office and situation to situation. Some of these different methods of calculation are shown in this publication.

It is not possible, however, in this book to explore all of these methods and there may have to be some interpolation from a method used here to one which you would want to use in a specific situation or circumstance. Some tasks in the landscape field are timeless. The time it requires to move bricks or the techniques for calculating the quantity of soil in a stockpile have not changed for thousands of years. Some of the materials used in contemporary landscape design and development are new and the weight and bulk of these materials need to be calculated by new techniques and methods. In many cases new methods or techniques have been developed to accomplish certain labor related functions and thus they take a lesser amount of time than it would have taken years ago. Many of these activities are translatable into current financial data at any time if the general hourly rates are known. In most cases this is what we have tried to give in this particular book.

In some cases newly developing equipment may be somewhat more expensive, but at the same time may be much more efficient. Some of the equipment figures in this particular publication may be outdated very quickly. As a result of all of the above, this book and its contents, are obviously not definitive. It has limits and is not totally complete. In some cases the information is not available. In other cases it might be available but we were not able to find it for use in this particular publication.

This book has roots and will surely have branches developing in years to come. There are a number of books that have been developed over the years dealing with methods and techniques for estimating or calculating the cost for landscape related operations and activities. There are many such publications in existence at the present time. A very limited number of these publications are listed in the Bibliography at the back of this particular book. The Surtees charts were developed in the 1920's, 30's and 40's and dealt mainly with the cost of activites in the nursery or in actual planting activities. The American Association of Nurserymen has developed an excellent guide to estimating landscape costs. The earlier book, **Off the Board/Into the Ground**, contained a section on estimating landscape costs as one-fourth of its areas of interest. Possibly one of the best books on this particular subject is the **Landscape Data Manual** developed by Professor James M. Griffin formerly of California Polytechnic Institute. More information on all of these books is contained at the back of this publication. Some materials have been adapted from those earlier studies. Some basic non-proprietary information may occur in this book as well as appearing in these earlier studies. This is not meant to constitute infringement in any way on those particular studies, but has been done to make this book as definitive and self-contained as possible. There is a great need for this type of information by a great many people including owners, designers and contractors or constructors.

Many aspects of landscape development are so inexact that it is difficult with any degree of certainty to estimate exactly landscape related time, supplies and materials. It is much more difficult in dealing with landscape or site related activities than it is in relationship to buildings or engineering structures.

This publication is an attempt to provide basic data and material in an easy to use form and format. Hopefully this book will be kept up-to-date and expanded in subsequent years. It is by no means definitive. **A GUIDE TO ESTIMATING LANDSCAPE COSTS is an attempt to provide basic data to make landscape estimates more accurate, more easily accomplished and more meaningful.**

The Center for Landscape Architectural Education and Research Reston, Virginia

contents

PERSONNEL TIME AND LABOR REQUIREMENTS

DISPOSAL OF EXCAVATED MATERIALS
MANHOURS PER HUNDRED (100) CUBIC YARDS

Truck Capacity and Length of Haul	Manhours								
	Average Speed 10 Mph			Average Speed 15 Mph			Average Speed 20 Mph		
	Truck Driver	Labor	Total	Truck Driver	Labor	Total	Truck Driver	Labor	Total
3 cu. yd. Truck									
1 Mile Haul	15.0	2.8	17.8	11.6	2.8	14.4	10.5	2.8	13.3
2 Mile Haul	21.8	2.8	24.6	16.2	2.8	19.0	14.0	2.8	16.8
3 Mile Haul	28.2	3.0	31.2	20.6	3.0	23.6	17.3	3.0	20.3
4 Mile Haul	36.0	3.0	39.0	26.8	3.0	29.8	21.0	3.0	24.0
5 Mile Haul	41.7	2.5	44.2						
4 cu. yd. Truck									
1 Mile Haul	11.3	2.1	13.4	8.8	2.0	10.8	7.9	2.1	9.0
2 Mile Haul	16.2	2.1	18.3	12.0	2.0	14.0	10.4	2.1	12.5
3 Mile Haul	21.6	2.0	23.6	15.8	2.3	18.1	13.2	2.2	15.4
4 Mile Haul	26.4	2.0	28.4	18.7	2.3	21.0	15.6	2.2	17.8
5 Mile Haul	31.3	1.3	32.6						
5 cu. yd. Truck									
1 Mile Haul	9.0	1.7	10.7	7.0	1.7	8.7	6.3	1.6	7.9
2 Mile Haul	13.0	1.7	14.7	9.7	1.7	11.4	8.3	1.7	10.0
3 Mile Haul	17.1	1.8	18.9	12.3	1.8	14.1	10.4	1.7	12.1
4 Mile Haul	21.0	2.0	23.0	15.0	2.0	17.0	12.4	1.7	14.1
5 Mile Haul	25.0	1.7	26.7						
8 cu. yd. Truck									
1 Mile Haul	5.6	1.0	6.6	4.8	1.0	5.8	4.0	1.0	5.0
2 Mile Haul	8.2	1.0	9.2	6.0	1.0	7.0	5.2	1.0	6.2
3 Mile Haul	10.5	1.1	11.6	7.8	1.1	8.9	6.5	1.0	7.5
4 Mile Haul	13.2	1.1	14.3	9.2	1.1	10.3	7.6	1.0	8.6
5 Mile Haul	15.6	1.3	16.9						

Manhours include round trip for truck driver, spotting at both ends, unloading and labor for minor repairs.

Manhours do not include labor for excavation or loading of trucks.

PERSONNEL TIME AND LABOR REQUIREMENTS

ESTIMATING UNIT PLANTING COSTS

These costs may vary considerably depending upon the type of soil encountered, the size of the order and the distance from the nursery. These are approximate cost prices to be used as a guide only. Planting costs include the required topsoil, fertilizer, mulching, peat, guying, pruning, etc.

Insert your own prices in the blank right hand column.

UNIT PLANTING COST OF DWARF AND SPREADING TYPE EVERGREENS: FURNISHED BALLED AND BURLAPPED

Size of Plant	Size of Hole	App. Soil Req.	With New Soil & Mulch
12-18 in.	18″ x 12″	1/2 bu.	
18-24 in.	20″ x 12″	3/4 bu.	
24-30 in.	22″ x 12″	1 bu.	
30-36 in.	24″ x 15″	1 bu.	
3-4 ft.	30″ x 15″	2 bu.	
4-5 ft.	42″ x 18″	5 bu.	
5-6 ft.	48″ x 18″	8 bu.	

LAWN CONSTRUCTION COSTS

Lawns of: **Your Price**

100 to   500 square feet

500 to 10,000 square feet

10,000 to 20,000 square feet

Over 20,000 square feet

Machine finished lawn — large areas

PERSONNEL TIME AND LABOR REQUIREMENTS

UNIT PLANTINGS COST OF UPRIGHT EVERGREENS AND BALLED AND BURLAPPED TREES FURNISHED BY NURSERY B & B GUYING AND MULCHING INCLUDED

Size of Plant	Size of Hole	App. Soil Req.	With New Soil & Mulch
12-18 in.	18″ x 12″	1/2 bu.	
18-24 in.	20″ x 12″	3/4 bu.	
2 - 3 ft.	24″ x 15″	1 bu.	
3 - 4 ft.	28″ x 18″	1 1/2 bu.	
4 - 5 ft.	32″ x 18″	2 bu.	
5 - 6 ft.	36″ x 18″	3 bu.	
6 - 7 ft. 1 - 1 1/4 in. Cal.	42″ x 22″	6 bu.	
7 - 8 ft. 1 1/4 - 1 1/2 in. Cal.	45″ x 22″	8 bu.	
8 - 10 ft. 1 1/2 - 2 in. Cal.	48″ x 24″	10 bu.	
2 - 2 1/2 in. Cal.	54″ x 24″	15 bu.	
2 1/2 - 3 in. Cal.	60″ x 24″	20 bu.	
3 - 3 1/2 in. Cal.	66″ x 24″	25 bu.	
3 1/2 - 4 in. Cal.	72″ x 24″	35 bu.	
4 - 4 1/2 in. Cal.	78″ x 30″	50 bu.	

UNIT PLANTING COST OF SHRUBS AND TREES FURNISHED
BARE ROOT NURSERY. THIS INCLUDES FRUIT TREES

Size of Plant	Size of Hole	App. Soil Req.	With New Soil & Mulch
15 - 18 in.	15″ x 12″	1/4 bu.	
18 - 24 in.	18″ x 12″	1/2 bu.	
2 - 3 ft.	18″ x 15″	3/4 bu.	
3 - 4 ft.	18″ x 18″	1 bu.	
4 - 5 ft.	24″ x 18″	1 1/4 bu.	
5 - 6 ft.	28″ x 18″	1 1/2 bu.	
6 - 8 ft.	30″ x 18″	3 bu.	
8 - 10 ft.	32″ x 18″	4 bu.	
10 - 12 ft.	36″ x 18″	6 bu.	
1 1/2 - 2 in. Cal.	38″ x 18″	7 bu.	
2 - 2 1/2 in. Cal.	40″ x 24″	9 bu.	
2 1/2 - 3 in. Cal.	42″ x 24″	10 bu.	

SALARY TABLE
(Based on a 40-hour week and an even 52-week year)

Per Year	Per Month	Per Week	Per Hour	Per Year	Per Month	Per Week	Per Hour
5,200.00	433.33	100.00	2.50	6,760.00	563.33	130.00	3.25
5,304.00	442.00	102.00	2.55	6,968.00	580.67	134.00	3.35
5,408.00	450.67	104.00	2.60	7,072.00	589.33	133.00	3.40
5,512.00	459.33	106.00	2.65	7,176.00	598.00	138.00	3.45
5,616.00	468.00	108.00	2.70	7,280.00	606.67	140.00	3.50
5,720.00	476.67	110.00	2.75	7,384.00	615.33	142.00	3.55
5,824.00	485.33	112.00	2.80	7,488.00	624.00	144.00	3.60
5,928.00	494.00	114.00	2.85	7,592.00	632.67	146.00	3.65
6,032.00	502.67	116.00	2.90	7,696.00	641.33	148.00	3.70
6,136.00	511.33	118.00	2.95	7,800.00	650.00	150.00	3.75
6,240.00	520.00	120.00	3.00	7,904.00	658.67	152.00	3,80
6,344.00	528.67	122.00	3.05	8,008.00	667.33	154.00	3.85
6,448.00	537.33	124.00	3.10	8,112.00	676.00	156.00	3.90
6,552.00	546.00	126.00	3.15	8,216.00	684.67	158.00	3.95
6,656.00	554.67	128.00	3.20	8,320.00	693.00	160.00	4.00

PERSONNEL TIME AND LABOR REQUIREMENTS

SALARY TABLE
Based on a 40-hour week and an even 52-week year

(continued)

Per Year	Per Month	Per Week	Per Hour	Per Year	Per Month	Per Week	Per Hour
8,424.00	702.00	162.00	4.05	12,584.00	1,048.67	242.00	6.05
8,528.00	710.67	164.00	4.10	12,688.00	1.057.34	244.00	6.10
8,632.00	719.33	166.00	4.15	12,792.00	1,066.00	246.00	6.15
8,736.00	728.00	168.00	4.20	12,896.00	1,074.66	248.00	6.20
8,840.00	736.67	170.00	4.25	13,000.00	1,083.34	250.00	6.25
8,944.00	745.33	172.00	4.30	13.104.00	1,092.00	252.00	6.30
9,048.00	754.00	174.00	4.35	13.208.00	1,100.67	254.00	6.35
9,152.00	762.67	176.00	4.40	13,312.00	1,109.34	256.00	6.40
9,256.00	771.33	178.00	4.45	13,416.00	1,118.00	258.00	6.45
9,360.00	780.00	180.00	4.50	13,520.00	1,126.66	260.00	6.50
9,464.00	788.67	182.00	4.55	13,624.00	1,135.33	262.00	6.55
9,568.00	797.33	184.00	4.60	13,728.0C	1,144.00	264.U0	6.60
9,672.00	806.00	186.00	4.65	13,832.00	1,152.67	266.00	6.65
9,776.00	814.67	188.00	4.70	13,936.00	1,161.34	268.00	6.70
9,880.00	823.33	190.00	4.75	14,040.00	1,170.00	270.00	6.75
9,984.00	832.00	192.00	4 80	14,144.00	1,178.66	272.00	6.80
10,088.00	840.67	194.00	4.85	14,248.00	1,187.33	274.00	6.85
10,192.00	849.33	196.00	4.90	14,352.00	1,196.00	276.00	6.90
10,296.00	858.00	198.00	4.95	14,456.00	1,204.67	278.00	6.95
10,400.00	866.66	200.00	5.00	14,560.00	1,213.34	280.00	7.00
10,504.00	875.27	202.00	5.05	14,664.00	1,222.00	282.00	7.05
10,608.00	884.00	204.00	5.10	14,768.00	1,230.66	284.00	7.10
10,712.00	892.67	206.00	5.15	14,872.00	1,239.33	286.00	7.15
10,816.00	901.34	208.00	5.20	14,976.00	1,248.00	288.00	7.20
10,920.00	910.00	210.00	5.25	15,000.00	1,256.67	790.00	7.25
11.024.00	918.66	212.00	5.30	15,104.00	1,265.34	292.00	7.30
11,128.00	927.34	214.00	5.35	15,208.00	1,274.00	294.00	7.35
11,232.00	936.00	216.00	5.40	15,312.00	1,282.66	296.00	7.40
11,336.00	944.67	218.00	5.45	15,416.00	1,291.33	298.00	7.45
11,440.00	953.34	220.00	5.50	15,520.00	1,300.00	300.00	7.50
11,544.00	962.00	222.00	5.55	15,624.00	1,308.67	302.00	7.55
11,648.00	970.66	224.00	5.60	15,728.00	1,317.34	304.00	7.60
11,752.00	979.34	226.00	5.65	15,832.00	1,326.00	306.00	7.65
11,856.00	988.00	228.00	5.70	15,936.00	1,334.66	308.00	7.70
11,960.00	996.67	230.00	5.75	16,040.00	1,343.34	310.00	7.75
12,064.00	1,005.34	232.00	5.80	16,144.00	1,352.00	312.00	7.80
12,168.00	1,014.00	234.00	5.85	16,248.00	1,360.67	314.00	7.85
12,272.00	1,022.66	236.00	5.90	16,352.00	1,369.34	316.00	7.90
12,376.00	1,031.34	238.00	5.95	16,456.00	1,378.00	318.00	7.95
12,480.00	1,040.00	240.00	6.00	16,640.00	1,386.00	320.00	8.00

PERSONNEL TIME AND LABOR REQUIREMENTS

ROCK EXCAVATION
MANHOURS PER UNITS LISTED

Type Rock	Operation	Unit	Manhours				
			Labor	Air Tool Oper.	Oper. Engr.	Powder Man	Total
Soft	Drilling Holes						
	2½'' with jackhammer	lin. ft.	.06	.06	.06		.18
	2'' with jackhammer	lin. ft.	.04	.04	.04		.12
	2'' with wagon drill	lin. ft.	.01		.07		.08
	Blasting	cu. yd.	.04			.02	.06
Medium	Drilling Holes						
	2½'' with jackhammer	lin. ft.	.08	.08	.08		.24
	2'' with jackhammer	lin. ft.	.07	.07	.07		.21
	2'' with wagon drill	lin. ft.	.03		.10		.13
	Blasting	cu. yd.	.06			.02	.08
Hard	Drilling Holes						
	2½'' with jackhammer	lin. ft.	.10	.10	.10		.30
	2'' with jackhammer	lin. ft.	.09	.09	.09		.27
	2'' with wagon drill	lin. ft.	.05		.15		.20
	Blasting	cu. yd.	.09			.04	.13

Manhours are for the above operations for primary blasting only. If secondary blasting is required and this same method is used, increase above manhours 50 percent.

Manhours do not include loading or hauling of blasted materials.

TYPICAL COST ESTIMATES

HICKS YEW HEDGE 3' HIGH
(Taxus media hicksi)

Hedge 100' long. Poor Soil.

Use plants 2½ - 3' high, balled and burlapped, trimmed down to 2½' after planting. Plant in single rows on 2½' centers. Ball 21'' x 18''. Trench 2½' wide x 2' deep. Topsoil to be premixed, in proportion of 4 parts of topsoil to one part humus.

40 Taxus media hicksi B & B 2½ - 3'		@ $20.00 (Retail)		$ 800.00
Trench 100 x 2½ x 2 = 500 x 20% = 600 cu. ft.				
Digging (20 cu. ft. per hr.)	30 hrs.	4.50	$135.00	
Backfilling (60 cu. ft. per hr.)	10 hrs.	4.50	45.00	
Planting (10 plants per hr.)	4 hrs.	4.50	18.00	
Trimming (20 plants per hr.)	2 hrs.	4.50	9.00	
Foreman (over 5 men)	9 hrs.	5.25	47.25	
			254.25	
Overhead 100%			254.25	
			508.50	
Profit 10%			50.85	559.35
				$1,359.35
Premixed topsoil	600 cu. ft.			
Less ball displacement (40 x 3.15)	126 cu. ft.			
	474 cu. ft.			
Topsoil	380 cu. ft.	14 cu. yds.	6.00	84.00	
Humus	94 cu. ft.	3½ cu. yds.	8.00	28.00	
			112.00	
Overhead 25%			28.00	140.00
				1,499.35
Profit 10%				149.94
				$1,649.29

Cost per plant   **$41.23**
Cost per linear foot   **$16.49**

TYPICAL FORM FOR CHECK OFF LIST FOR ESTIMATING JOBS

	Quantity	Unit Cost		Subtotal		Total	

1. Survey of property

2. Initial cleanup or clearing site
   Salvage of desirable elements and
   storage

3. Grading (excavating, backfill,
   leveling)
   a.
   b.

4. Construction
   a. Buildings, bathhouse, lath,
      utility shelter)
      (1)
      (2) Staining or painting

   b. Fences and screens
      (1)
      (2) Staining or painting

   c. Seats and benches
      (1)
      (2) Staining or painting

   d. Walls (concrete, masonry,
      bulkhead, retaining)
      (1) Footings and forming
      (2)

   g. Paving (walks, pads, patio,
      driveway, parking, courts)
      (1) Concrete—Type
      (2) Acid staining or painting
      (3) Tanbark, gravel, crusher run
      (4) Masonry—Type
      (5) Coloring

   h. Headers—lawn, cement, asphalt
      (1)

5. Electrical
   a. Leadin, wall plugs, conduit,
      switches, lights, lamps

PERSONNEL TIME AND LABOR REQUIREMENTS

9

	Quantity	Unit Cost	Subtotal	Total
6. Irrigation (sprinklers, hose bibbs, fountains, Feed lines, control valves) a. b. c.				
7. Drainage (drain tile, catch basins, drain rock) a. b.				
8. Soil conditioning (peat, manure, shavings, fertilizer, topsoil, rototiil, leveling, spreading, fine grading) a. b. c. d.				
9. Plant material per plant list a. Plants b. Planting labor c. Tree stakes d. Lawn e. Misc. — ties, guy wire				
10. Maintenance (watering, weeding, mowing) a. b.				
11. Garden accessories (movable plant boxes, benches, lights and switches, fire bowls, art pieces)				
12. Replacement of desirable existing elements				
13. Supervision				
14. Final cleanup				
15. Contingency				

PERSONNEL TIME AND LABOR REQUIREMENTS

(C) Construction
    (1) Concrete
        (a) Estimating
        (b) Layout and supervision
        (c) Excavating
        (d) Fine grade
            (1) Banks
            (2) Slab
        (e) Forming
            (1) Slabs and expansion joints
            (2) Walls
            (3) Footings
        (f) Grids
        (g) Placing concrete
        (h) Finishing
            (1) Exposed aggregate
            (2) Exposed seeded aggregate
            (3) Place color
            (4) Place non-skid or sparkle
            (5) Sacking walls
            (6) Grinding
            (7) Grouting
        (i) Strip
        (j) Clean-up
        (k) Demolition
        (z) _____

    (2) Carpentry
        (a) Estimating
        (b) Layout and supervision
        (c) Benches
            (1) Build bench
            (2) Setting legs including placing concrete or compacting
            (3) Bolting
         (d) Headerboard
            (1) 1 x 4   (5) 1 x 4 laminated
            (2) 2 x 4   (6) 2 x 4 laminated
            (3) 2 x 6   (7) 2 x 6 laminated
            (4) 2 x 8   (8) 2 x 8 laminated
        (e) Fencing
            (1) Digging holes
            (2) Setting posts
            (3) Building frame
            (4) Placing siding
                (a) Grapestakes 1″ x 1″
                (b) Grapestakes 2″ x 2″
                (c) Other
                (d) Cap

(f) Decks
- (1) Setting piers
- (2) Placing bolts
- (3) Building deck

    (g) Framing (walls, etc.)

    (h) Bulkheads
- (1) Dig holes for post
- (2) Setting posts
- (3) Building frame
- (4) Place siding
- (5) Place cap
- (6) Backfill

    (i) Clean-up

    (j) Painting

(3) Grading and excavation
- (a) Estimating
- (b) Layout and supervision
- (c) Fill
  - (1) Place by hand
  - (2) Place by machine
  - (3) Haul fill or topsoil
- (d) Excavate
  - (1) Hand
  - (2) Jackhammer
  - (3) Machine
  - (4) Pits or box areas
- (e) Compaction
  - (1) Hand
  - (2) Machine
- (f) Trenching
  - (1) Hand
  - (2) Machine
- (g) Clean-up
- (h) Grading
  - (1) Machine
  - (2) Hand

(4) Drainage
- (a) Layout and supervision
- (b) Trenching
  - (1) Hand
  - (2) Machine

    (c) Laying tile or pipe

    (d) Placing drain rock

    (e) Placing catch basins

    (f) Backfill

    (g) Down spouts (typing in)

    (h) Clean-up

(5) Miscellaneous

    (a) Masonry

        (1) Trench and pour footing

        (2) Place material

            (a) Brick in sand or mortar

            (b) Flagstone in sand or mortar

            (c) Concrete block in sand or mortar

            (d) Bowls or rock in grout

    (b) Walkways, driveways, roads, tracks, etc.

        (1) Excavate

        (2) Fill and compact

        (3) Headerboards

        (4) Place and compact base

        (5) Place and compact final course (red rock, asphalt, etc.)

    (c) Place large stones or rocks

(I) Irrigation

    (1) Estimating

        (a) Actual costing or take-off

        (b) View site

        (c) Plan design

        (d) Material procurement

    (2) Layout

    (3) Machine trench

    (4) Hand trench or clean trench

    (5) Horizontal boring

    (6) Installation of pipe

        (a) Galvanized pipe

        (b) Copper pipe

        (c) Plastic pipe

        (d) Automatic controls

    (7) Backfill

        (a) Machine

        (b) Hand

        (c) Mechanical compaction

        (d) Sodding operations

(8) Lower Heads
(9) Repair Damaged Heads
(10) Adjust
(11) Pool Mechanics
(12) Hook-ups to existing lines
(z) _____

(P) Planting
    (1) Estimating
    (2) Layout and supervision
    (3) Hand work
        (a) Lawn areas
        (b) Planting areas
        (c) Ground cover areas
        (d) Weed removal
    (4) Ground preparation
        (a) Spread fertilizer, etc.
        (b) Ripping
        (c) Rotovating
        (d) Rototilling
        (e) Discing
        (f) Harrowing
        (g) Dragging
    (5) Digging holes
        (a) 1 gal.
        (b) 5 gal.
        (c) 6 gal.
        (d) 15 gal.
        (e) Box or specimen tree up to 36 inches
        (f) Box or specimen tree over 36 inches
    (6) Planting
        (a) 1 gal. or pots
        (b) 5 gal.
        (c) 15 gal.
        (d) Box or specimen trees up to 36 inches
        (e) Box or specimen trees over 36 inches
        (f) Ground cover
        (g) Ice plant cuttings
        (h) Seeding of lawns or field
        (i) Staking and guying
            (1) Single stakes
            (2) Double stakes

(7) Watering
(8) Clean-up
(9) Demolition
(z) ——————

(M) Maintenance
(1) Estimating
(2) Layout and supervision
(3) Watering
(4) Weed control spray
(5) Weed control cultivating
(6) Fertilizing
(7) Pest and fungus control
(8) Mowing of lawns
(9) Pruning
(10) Reseeding
(11) Clean-up

(O) Overhead
(1) Maintenance of equipment
(2) Maintenance of yard and miscellaneous
(3) Purchasing and delivery of material

EXCAVATION BY HAND LABOR WITH WHEELBARROWS
(AVERAGE BARROW LOAD ASSUMED AS 2 CU. FT.)

Soil	Loosen and Load, Min.	Cu. Yd. per Man per Hr.			Labor-hours per Cu. Yd.		
		Haul 50 Ft.	Haul 100 Ft.	Haul 150 Ft.	Haul 50 Ft.	Haul 100 Ft.	Haul 150 Ft.
Light (sand)	1.5–3.0	1.12–1.80	0.90–1.28	0.75–1.00	0.56–0.89	0.78–1.11	1.00–1.33
Medium (loam)	2.0–4.0	0.90–1.50	0.75–1.12	0.64–0.90	0.67–1.11	0.89–1.33	1.11–1.56
Heavy (clay)	2.5–5.0	0.75–1.28	0.64–1.00	0.56–0.82	0.78–1.33	1.00–1.56	1.22–1.78
Hard pan	3.0–6.0	0.64–1.12	0.56–0.90	0.50–0.75	0.89–1.56	1.11–1.78	1.33–2.00

LOOSENING SOIL: PICK & SHOVEL

Cubic Yards/Hours			Hours/Cubic Yard		
Medium Soil	Heavy Soil	Hard Pan	Medium Soil	Heavy Soil	Hard Pan
2–4	1–3	.5–1.5	.25–.50	.33–1.0	.67–2.0

EXCAVATION PER CUBIC YARD

Ordinary Soil		Average cu. yds. per eight-hour day using a fifty-minute hour		
		Tractor *	Hrs. **	***
Plowing and loosening soil	280-320	8	8	.025
Drag scraper excavation	Move 100' to dump 20-25	8	8	.375
Dig, shovel and load by hand	5-8	—	—	1.375
Trenches 4-5' deep, hand labor	4-5	—	—	1.75
Pits and holes to 6' deep	4	—	—	2.00
Backfill by hand	16-18	—	—	.47
Spread soil or other loose material by hand	40-48	—	—	.18

TYPICAL SOIL MOVING—HAND LABOR

Operation	Cu. Yds./8 Hr. Day	Hrs./Cu. Yd.
Dig and Load with shovel (loose)	5–8	1.60–1.00
Trench 4' to 5' deep	4–5	2.00–1.60
Pits and Holes to 6' deep	3–4	2.67–2.00
Backfill by Hand	16–18	0.50–0.44
Spread soil or other loose material	40–48	0.20–0.17
Shoveling and grading	4–6	2.00–1.33

ACTUAL VALUE CAN BE FIGURED FROM PLANTING COSTS, ANNUAL EXPENSES AND LAND REHABILITATION

A formula has been developed to find the actual value of trees that may have been destroyed or damaged, or are to be condemned because of land use change. This formula covers the costs involved in establishing and maintaining the planting. It does not include intrinsic or sentimental values. The formula is composed of three parts:

1. Planting costs, amortized for the duration of the planting. This includes the cost of the ground preparation, the trees and the labor of planting.

2. Annual expenses and their amortization for the period involved. Among these expenses are cultivation, spraying, pruning, taxes on the land and interest on the land investment.

3. Land rehabilitation. This is the expense incurred where labor has to be expended to remove killed or excessively damaged trees. Thus, the land can be put back into approximately as good a condition as it was originally. This cost will not always be a factor in the value computations.

In its simplest equation form, the formula can be stated as:

$$V = P + (P \times C) + (\frac{E}{R} \times C) + L$$

V = Value of the tree (or trees).
P = Planting costs. This should include the ground preparation and actual planting, as well as the cost of the tree. If you did the work yourself, you are entitled to a reasonable wage.
C = Compound interest factor. The interest rate should be based on investment return, not the rate that must be paid if you borrow. Currently a 10 percent interest rate is considered fair. This compound interest rate is compounded for the age of the planting. These compound interest factors can be obtained from tables from your banker or insurance agent.
E = Annual expenses. Included here are taxes on the land, interest on land investment (here for convenience sake you use the current interest rate)/cultivation, watering, pruning, fertilizing, insect and disease control and other recurring jobs. These expenses include labor as well as material outlay.
R = Annual interest rate in the decimal system (10 percent as .10).
L = Land rehabilitation charges, where applicable. This would include the cutting down of the tree and the digging of the stump, including the disposal of the debris.

APPLYING THE FORMULA . . .

As an example, let's assume a ten-year-old spruce tree on one corner of a lot was broken off by vandals. Let s put the cost data into the formula.

P = $250.00   This includes the tree and the planting costs.
C = $ 10.00   This is the compound interest factor for 10 years at .10.
E = $ 32.35   In this recurring expense there are the following charges:
          $ 4.50   watering
          $ 4.50   cultivation
          $ 5.35   pruning
          $ 1.00   taxes on area involved—9 sq. ft. or 1/800 of a 50' x 150' lot, with $800.00 land tax
          $10.00   land investment lot cost—$10,200.00
          $ 7.00   insect and disease spray

R = .10
L = $100.00   Digging out the stump and disposing of same.

Using the above costs in the formula, it would work out this way:

$$V = P + (P \times C) + (\frac{E}{R} \times C) + L$$

$$V = \$250 + (\$250 \times \$10.00) + (\frac{\$32.35}{.10} \times \$10.00) + \$100.00$$

$$V = \$2,907.35$$

If you will study the formula closely, you will notice that the tree value hinges very much on the annual expenses. This unit takes into consideration the location where it is planted and also the person's interest in this tree. If this portion of the formula is not honestly valued, then you will obtain a valuation that is not a true reflection of the costs incurred in growing this tree.

Keep in mind that this formula does not take into consideration any intrinsic values, only those actually incurred, and which can usually be proven.

As in other formulas, this one has limitations. A 200-year-old tree, past maturity, certainly would be way over priced, and common sense will have to be used in deciding on its final value. What is described here is an aid, not an answer to all problems.

This is merely one method of calculating the intrinsic value of trees. There are many other methods and techniques. For more information on this in any geographic area it is suggested that the reader contact local colleges or universities, cooperative extension service agents or forestry or shade tree associations.

TIME REQUIREMENTS OF TYPICAL LANDSCAPE OPERATIONS

Excavation by hand: One man can excavate 5 to 6 cu. yds. in 8 hrs., earth thrown to one side.

Loading trucks: One man can load from ground 7 cu. yds. earth on a 7 yd. truck in 2-1/2 hrs., freshly loosened. Compacted or frozen earth, 2 to 3 times as long.

Excavation: Capacity 3/4 cu. yds. shovel will excavate 250 cu. yds. in 8 hrs.
  Add cost of whatever number of men are required to follow the shovel for trimming, etc. An acre of ground to be excavated 12 inches deep will take 62 hours, plus time of installing and removing of shovel. The time includes loading directly on the trucks for removal of debris. Figure 20% for expansion.

Removal of debris: To haul one load of 7 cu. yds. to a dump one mile away will take 3/4 hour for truck and driver.

Plowing: One acre of ground can be plowed by team of 2 horses and driver in 10 hours, once over. Tractor and operator in 3-1/2 hours.

Cultivation: One acre of ground can be cultivated by one horse and driver in 5 hours, average.

HOURS FOR TRANSPLANTING LARGE TREE

MAN/HOUR REQUIREMENTS

Cost Records Indicate the Following Man/Hours for this Operation

Preparatory work: — Man/Hours

Assembly of tools, equipment and necessary materials 10½
Digging tree, lacing root ball and dozing out ramp for lowboy . . . . . . .3 men-8 hrs 24
Loading tree at nursery . . . . .5 men-7 hrs 35
Foreman 8

Digging hole and ramp at planting site, backfilling hole with
  good planting soil, and compacting firmly . . . . .1 man 3½
Moving and unloading tree and securing temporary guys . . . . .5 men-8 hrs 40
Foreman 8

Laying down permanent drainage system to prevent over-
  watering of tree, backfilling, watering, attaching perma-
  nent guys, and mulching . . . . .2 men-8 hrs 16

_____

145

Preparatory work: — Man/Hours

(It must be noted that the planting crew was unfamiliar with the method used on this large tree. It is estimated that a maximum of 110-120 man/hours would be required to duplicate a similar operation.)

TIME REQUIRED TO PUT DOWN 1 IN. OF
WATER ON 1,500 SQ. FT. LAWN

For various hose diameters
at 50 psi water pressure

HOSE I.D.	GALS. per min.	TIME
7/16"	7.3	2 HRS. 8 MIN.
1/2"	10.9	1 HR. 26 MIN.
5/8"	15.1	1 HR. 2 MIN.
3/4"	26.8	35 MIN.

LABOR REQUIRED (APPROX.)
INSTALLATION CONCRETE WALKS
PER 100 SQUARE FEET

Activity	Min. Hrs.	Max. Hrs.
Level and Tamp Subsoil:	.5	2.0
Place, Level and Tamp Subbase:	.5	2.0
Place Forms and Screeds:	.5	2.0
Mix and Place Concrete:	1.5	3.0
Finish	1.0	3.0
Cure, Remove Forms, Clean Up:	.5	2.0
	4.5	14.0

*TIME DATA: PLANTING TREES AND SHRUBS NURSERY CONTAINER STOCK
(INCLUDED OPERATIONS: DIG HOLE, SPOT AND CUT CONTAINER, MIX BACKFILL, PLANT AND BASIN.)

Container Size	Minutes per Plant	Crew Size	Plants per Hour
1 gal.	12	1	5.0
5 gal.	30	1	2.0
10 gal.	40	1	1.5
15 gal.	90	2	0.67
24″ Box	260	2	0.17
30″ Box	720	3	0.08

*Data is from rough approximation. Many variables will be encountered.

*TIME DATA: TRANSPLANTING FIELD GROWN STOCK: ALL OPERATIONS
(DIG, WRAP, TRANSPLANT)

Ball Size (Cu. Ft.)	Approx. Ball Weight (lbs.)	Approx. Time (Hrs. per Plant)
1	80	1.5
2	160	2.0
4	320	4.0
8	640	8.0
12	960	10.0
20	1600	18.0
36	2880	34.0
48	3840	44.0
60	4800	55.0
68	5440	60.0
90	7200	80.0

*Above are rough approximations. Differences in soils, plants and type equipment a few of the variables.

EXAMPLES OF MAN/HOUR RATES FOR LANDSCAPE OPERATIONS

There should be several sets of charts in planting operation, for instance, showing varying conditions under which plant material might be planted. Some plantings may be in prepared beds, others may be where fill soil will have to be excavated and new topsoil put in around the plants; then too, a large pine tree or a large spreading juniper will require more time to handle the plant than a large arborvitae. All these things should be considered, so in two extreme planting conditions, the charts for evergreen, shrub and tree planting would look like this: (other charts might be made for degrees of operations between these extremes.)

EVERGREEN PLANTING CHART

Dwarf & Spreading Type (Actual Planting on Jobs)			Upright Type (Actual Planting on Jobs)		
Size	In prepared beds— water, cleanup, outline	Spade or remove sod, excavate subsoil. Add topsoil, cleanup, outline	Size	In prepared beds— water, cleanup, outline	Spade or remove sod, excavate subsoil. Add topsoil, cleanup, outline
18–24"	.3 hr.	.42 hr.	18–24"	.25 hr.	.4 hr.
2–2-1/2'	.4 hr.	.6 hr.	2–2-1/2'	.3 hr.	.5 hr.
2-1/2–3'	.5 hr.	.85 hr.	2-1/2–3'	.4 hr.	.7 hr.
3–3-1/2'	.7 hr.	1.0 hr.	3–3-1/2'	.5 hr.	.85 hr.
3-1/2–4'	.9 hr.	1.5 hrs.	3-1/2–4'	.65 hr.	1.0 hr.
4–5'	1.5 hrs.	2.3 hrs.	4–5'	.9 hr.	1.5 hr.
5–6'	2.3 hrs.	3.8 hrs.	5–6'	1.25 hrs.	2.3 hrs.
Etc.			Etc.		

SHRUB PLANTING CHART

Shrubs & Dwarf Trees Bare Root (Actual Planting on Jobs)			Shrubs & Dwarf Trees Balled & Burlapped (Actual Planting on Jobs)		
Size	Prepared Beds	Spade, etc.	Size	Prepared Beds	Spade, etc.
18–24"	.2 hr.	.3 hr.	18–24"	.3 hr.	.42 hr.
2–3'	.25 hr.	.42 hr.	2–3'	.42 hr.	.6 hr.
3–4'	.33 hr.	.5 hr.	3–4'	.66 hr.	.85 hr.
4–5'	.5 hr.	.7 hr.	4–5'	.8 hr.	1.0 hr.
5–6'	.66 hr.	.85 hr.	5–6'	1.0 hr.	1.25 hrs.
Etc.			Etc.		

Ball Size Dia. Depth (in.)	Cu. Ft. of Soil in Ball	Wt. of Ball (lbs.)	Time to Dig & Lace (min.)	Time to Handle Ball (min.)	Size Hole Req. (in.)	Cu. Ft. Soil Hole, to Excavate	Time to Dig Hole (min.)	Cu. Ft. Soil Dis-place-ment	Time to Plant & Prune (min.)	Time to Water, Wrap, Guy, & Clean Up (min.)	Cu. Ft. Topsoil Handled in Moving	Total Time in Moving
12x12	-7/10	56	15	10	24	3-3/4	20	3	15	4	10-1/2	64
18x16	2	160	30	20	30	7-1/2	28	5-1/2	21	5	21	1-2/3
24x18	4	320	60	40	36	13	65	9	49	12	38	3-2/3
30x21	7-1/2	600	114	76	48	26-1/2	133	19	100	25	76	7-1/3
36x24	12-1/2	980	189	126	54	38	190	25-1/2	143	36	114	11-1/3
42x27	19	1,520	285	190	66	64	320	45	240	60	185	18-1/2
48x30	28	2,040	420	280	72	85	360	57	270	68	254	23-1/3
54x33	38-1/2	3,060	579	386	84	127	635	88-1/2	476	119	370	36-1/2
60x36	52	4,160	780	520	90	159	795	107	596	149	474	47-1/3
66x39	68	5,440	1,020	680	96	196	905	128	679	168	596	57-1/2
72x42	87	7,160	1,305	870	108	267	1,240	180	930	233	795	76

(Dig hole, mix fertilizer, open can, plant and basin.)

3" & 4" pots	3 minutes per plant
Gal. cans	10 minutes per plant
5 gal. cans	25 minutes per plant
10 gal. cans	40 minutes per plant
15 gal. cans	90 minutes per plant
24" box (2 men)	3 hours per man
30" box (3 men)	4 hours per man

Stepping Stones of cement or flagstone
Figure 15 lin. ft. per hr.

Flagstrip or Lawn Curb
(Dig channel, lay and backfill) Man will install 15 lin. ft. per hr.

Redwood Rounds
(Excavate, throw soil to one side, place and level blocks and backfill) Man will lay 10 sq. ft. per hr.

Redwood Headers or Stripping 1 X 3
(Dig channel, stake, nail and backfill) Figure 20 ft. per hour

BREAKDOWN OF COSTS PER HOUR FOR LANDSCAPE CREWMEN

Base Rate

Present scale is $4.47 per hour $4.17*   *7.00*

Present scale ($4.47 per hr.) is equal to $2,210 for an 8½-hour day. The worker has a
potential of 2,210 working hours per year, before overtime.

Benefits Paid by Employer

Two weeks paid vacation totals 85 hours or $379.95 which amounts to 17.2 cents per
hour worked .... .172   *.27*

Six paid holidays equal 51 hours or $227.97 which amounts to 10.3 cents per hour worked ... .103   *.16*

Coffee breaks—two ten-minute breaks daily equals 82 hours per year which is
equivalent to $1.41 per day or 16.6 cents per hour worked .... .166   *.26*

Non-productive time—average of 15 min. lost time daily is equal to 61 hours
per year or 12.3 cents per hour .... .123   *.19*

Employer's Contributions

Employer's portion of F.I.C.A. (social security) @ 3.625% .... .162   *.25*

Federal unemployment tax @ 2.7% .... .121   *.19*

State unemployment tax @ 3.0% .... .134   *.21*

Union health and welfare benefits .... .062   *.10*

Workmen's compensation .... .135   *.20*

Other, such as liability and property damage .... .118   *.18*

Overhead

Paymaster
Management and office
Heat, light and telephone   equal to 18% of base rate or .... .805   *1.26*
Supervisory help
Non-productive time
Bonus or other gratuities

Trucks, Tools and Equipment

Capital investment
Depreciation   equal to 1.27 cents per hr/per man 1.270   *2.54*
Hand Tools

Total Cost **$7.841**   *12.81*

---

*Adjust pay rate scale for regional variations and normal increases in rate of pay over time
beyond that used in the illustration.

CONVERTING TIME INTO DOLLARS

Quick estimation of job costs will make bid preparation and budget planning more efficient. Check the Price Conversion Table to figure the total cost of the job. Use the column which equals the labor rate you charge or your employee pay scale. The conversion table also can be used to figure the cost of operating equipment by placing a dollar per hour cost on the use of the equipment. The table is based on tenths per hour or 0.1 for every 6 minutes; five-tenths or 0.5 equals 30 minutes of job time.

PRICE CONVERSION TABLE

Suggested Time (Hrs.)	\$2.50	\$3.00	\$3.50	\$4.00	\$4.50	\$5.00	\$5.50	\$6.00	\$6.50	\$7.00	\$7.50	\$8.00	\$8.50	\$9.00	\$9.50	\$10.00
							Labor Rate Per Hour									
0.1	0.25	0.30	0.35	0.40	0.45	0.50	0.55	0.60	0.65	0.70	0.75	0.80	0.85	0.90	0.95	1.00
0.2	0.50	0.60	0.70	0.80	0.90	1.00	1.10	1.20	1.30	1.40	1.50	1.60	1.70	1.80	1.90	2.00
0.3	0.75	0.90	1.05	1.20	1.35	1.50	1.65	1.80	1.95	2.10	2.25	2.40	2.55	2.70	2.85	3.00
0.4	1.00	1.20	1.40	1.60	1.80	2.00	2.20	2.40	2.60	2.80	3.00	3.20	3.40	3.60	3.80	4.00
0.5	1.25	1.50	1.75	2.00	2.25	2.50	2.75	3.00	3.25	3.50	3.75	4.00	4.25	4.50	4.75	5.00
0.6	1.50	1.80	2.10	2.40	2.70	3.00	3.30	3.60	3.90	4.20	4.50	4.80	5.10	5.40	5.70	6.00
0.7	1.75	2.10	2.45	2.80	3.15	3.50	3.85	4.20	4.55	4.90	5.25	5.60	5.95	6.30	6.65	7.00
0.8	2.00	2.40	2.80	3.20	3.60	4.00	4.40	4.80	5.20	5.60	6.00	6.40	6.80	7.20	7.60	8.00
0.9	2.25	2.70	3.15	3.60	4.05	4.50	4.95	5.40	5.85	6.30	6.75	7.20	7.65	8.10	8.55	9.00
1.0	2.50	3.00	3.50	4.00	4.50	5.00	5.50	6.00	6.50	7.00	7.50	8.00	8.50	9.00	9.50	10.00
2.0	5.00	6.00	7.00	8.00	9.00	10.00	11.00	12.00	13.00	14.00	15.00	16.00	17.00	18.00	19.00	20.00
3.0	7.50	9.00	10.50	12.00	13.50	15.00	16.50	18.00	19.50	21.00	22.50	24.00	25.50	27.00	28.50	30.00
4.0	10.00	12.00	14.00	16.00	18.00	20.00	22.00	24.00	26.00	28.00	30.00	32.00	34.00	36.00	38.00	40.00
5.0	12.50	15.00	17.50	20.00	22.50	25.00	27.50	30.00	32.50	35.00	37.50	40.00	42.50	45.00	47.50	50.00
6.0	15.00	18.00	21.00	24.00	27.00	30.00	33.00	36.00	39.00	42.00	45.00	48.00	51.00	54.00	57.00	60.00
7.0	17.50	21.00	24.50	28.00	31.50	35.00	38.50	42.00	45.50	49.00	52.50	56.00	59.50	63.00	66.50	70.00
8.0	20.00	24.00	28.00	32.00	36.00	40.00	44.00	48.00	52.00	56.00	60.00	64.00	68.00	72.00	76.00	80.00
9.0	22.50	27.00	31.50	36.00	40.50	45.00	49.50	54.00	58.50	63.00	67.50	72.00	76.50	81.00	85.50	90.00
10.0	25.00	30.00	35.00	40.00	45.00	50.00	55.00	60.00	65.00	70.00	75.00	80.00	85.00	90.00	95.00	100.00
20.0	50.00	60.00	70.00	80.00	90.00	100.00	110.00	120.00	130.00	140.00	150.00	160.00	170.00	180.00	190.00	200.00
30.0	75.00	90.00	105.00	120.00	135.00	150.00	165.00	180.00	195.00	210.00	225.00	240.00	255.00	270.00	285.00	300.00
40.0	100.00	120.00	140.00	160.00	180.00	200.00	220.00	240.00	260.00	280.00	300.00	320.00	340.00	360.00	380.00	400.00
50.0	125.00	150.00	175.00	200.00	225.00	250.00	275.00	300.00	325.00	350.00	375.00	400.00	425.00	450.00	475.00	500.00
60.0	150.00	180.00	210.00	240.00	270.00	300.00	330.00	360.00	390.00	420.00	450.00	480.00	510.00	540.00	570.00	600.00
70.0	175.00	210.00	245.00	280.00	315.00	350.00	385.00	420.00	455.00	490.00	525.00	560.00	595.00	630.00	665.00	700.00
80.0	200.00	240.00	280.00	320.00	360.00	400.00	440.00	480.00	520.00	560.00	600.00	640.00	680.00	720.00	760.00	800.00
90.0	225.00	270.00	315.00	360.00	405.00	450.00	495.00	540.00	585.00	630.00	675.00	720.00	765.00	810.00	855.00	900.00
100.0	250.00	300.00	350.00	400.00	450.00	500.00	550.00	600.00	650.00	700.00	750.00	800.00	850.00	900.00	950.00	1000.00

I. Grading Operations:
Area to Finish Grade

Loosen soil six inches deep:

Light soil:

Tractor will complete . . . . 2,700 sq. ft. per hour

Rototiller will complete . . . . 1,550 sq. ft. per hour

Hand labor will complete . . . . 63 sq. ft. per hour

Heavy soil:

Tractor wil complete . . . . 1,900 sq. ft. per hour

Rototiller will complete . . . . 700 sq. ft. per hour

Hand labor will complete . . . . 40 sq. ft. per hour

Bring loosened soil to rough grade:

Light soil:

Tractor will complete . . . . 1,850 sq. ft. per hour

Hand labor will complete . . . . 340 sq. ft. per hour

Heavy soils:

Tractor will complete . . . . 1,600 sq. ft. per hour

Hand labor will complete . . . . 250 sq. ft. per hour

Rough grade to finish grade:

Light soil:

1 man will finish grade . . . . 560 sq. ft. per hour

Heavy soil

1 man will finish grade . . . . 375 sq. ft. per hour

II. Installation of Finish Grade:
Turf Installation

A. Seed Installation:

Operation	Sq./Ft./Man Hr.
Hand Seeding:	5,400
Seed by knapsack spreader	15,000
Seed by 18'' spreader	6,720
Fertilization by 18'' spreader	6,720
Covering seed by raking	4,000
Top Dressing	2,500
Rolling light weight roller	4,000

B. Installation by Vegetative Parts:

	Spacing or Rate	Man Hrs./ 1000 Sq. Ft.
Plugging:	6'' o.c.	5.00
	12'' o.c.	1.50
Sprigging:	6'' o.c.	2.00
	12'' o.c.	0.75
Stolonization	2 bushel	0.50
	4 bushel	0.75
*Sodding	est. sod in strips	**4.5 to 6.5

*Assumes established Sub Grade.

**Variances: Proximity of Sod, Access to Area, degree of cutting/patching necessary.

ESTIMATED ANNUAL LOSS CAUSED BY FIVE MINUTE TIME WASTAGE
PER EMPLOYEE PER WORK DAY
(Based on 44 hour week, 255 working days/year. Overhead as equal to the hourly rate.)

Hourly Rate	Number of Employees					
	5	10	25	50	100	500
2.50	531.00	1,062.50	2,656.50	5,313.00	10,626.00	53,130.00
2.75	584.40	1,168.80	2,922.00	5,811.00	11,000.00	58,440.00
3.00	637.50	1,275.00	3,187.50	6,375.00	12,750.00	63,750.00
3.25	690.60	1,381.20	3,453.00	6,906.00	13,812.00	69,060.00
3.50	743.80	1,487.60	3,719.00	7,438.00	14,876.00	74,380.00
3.75	796.90	1,593.80	3,984.50	7,969.00	15,938.00	79,690.00
4.00	850.00	1,700.00	4,250.00	8,500.00	17,000.00	85,000.00
4.25	903.10	1,806.20	4,515.50	9.013.00	18,062.00	90,310.00
4.50	956.30	1,912.60	4,781.50	9,563.00	19,126.00	95,630.00
4.75	1.009.40	2,018.80	5,047.00	10,094.00	20,180.00	100,940.00
5.00	1,062.50	2,125.20	5,313.00	10,626;00	21,252.00	106,260.00
5.25	1,115.60	2,231.20	5,578.00	11,156.00	22,321.00	111,560.00
5.50	1,168.80	2,337.60	5,044.00	11,688.00	23,376.00	116,880.00
5.75	1,221.90	2,443.80	6,109.50	12,219.00	24,438.00	122,190.00
6.00	1,275.00	2,550.00	6,375.00	12,750.00	25,500.00	127,500.00
6.25	1,328.10	2,656.20	6,640.20	13,281.00	26,562.00	132,810.00
6.50	1,381.20	2,762.40	6,906.00	13,812.00	27,624.00	138,120.00
6.75	1,434.30	2,868.60	7,171.50	14,343.00	28,686.00	143,430.00
7.00	1,497.60	2,975.20	7,438.00	14,876.00	29,752.00	148,760.00
7.25	1,540.70	3,081.40	7,703.50	15.407.00	30,814.00	154,070.00
7.50	1,593.80	3,187.60	7,969.00	15.938.00	31,876.00	159,380.00
7.75	1,646.90	3,293.80	8,234.50	16,496.00	32,938.00	164,690.00
8.00	1,700.00	3,400.00	8,500.00	17,000.00	34,000.00	170,000.00
8.25	1,753.10	3,506.20	8,756.50	17,531.00	35,062.00	175,310.00
8.50	1,806.20	3,612.40	9,031.00	18,062.00	36,124.00	180,620.00
8.75	1,859.30	3,718.60	9,296.50	18,593.00	37,186.00	185,930.00
9.00	1,912.60	3,825.20	9,563.00	19,126.00	38,252.00	191,260.00
9.25	1,965.60	3,931.00	10,094.00	19.655.00	39,310.00	196,550.00
9.50	2,018.80	4,037.60	10,358.50	21,188.00	40,376.00	201,880.00
9.75	2,071.70	4,143.40	10,656.00	20717.00	41,434.00	207,170.00
10.00	2,125.20	4,262.40	10,891.50	21,312.00	42,624.00	213,120.00
10.25	2,178.20	4,356.60	11,156.00	21,738.00	43,566.00	217,830.00
10.50	2,231.20	4,462.40	11,420.50	22,312.00	44,624.00	223,120.00
10.75	2,284.10	4,658.20	11,688.00	22,841.00	45,682.00	228,410.00
11.00	2,337.60	4,675.20	11,951.50	23,376.00	46,752.00	233,760.00
11.25	2,390.30	4,780.60	12,219.00	23,903.00	47,806.00	239,030.00
11.50	2,443.80	4,887.60	12,494.50	24,438.00	48,876.00	244,380.00
11.75	2,496.90	4,993.80	12,750.00	24,969.00	49,938.00	249,690.00
12.00	2,550.00	5,100.00	13,015.50	25,550.00	51,000.00	255,000.00
12.25	2,603.10	5,206.20	12,281.00	26,031.00	52,062.00	260,310.00
12.50	2,656.20	5,312.40	12,546.50	26,562.00	53,124.00	265,620.00
12.75	2,709.30	5,418.60	13,546.50	27,093.00	54,186.00	270,930.00

PERSONNEL TIME AND LABOR REQUIREMENTS

PERSONNEL, TIME AND LABOR DEMANDS

AREA AND OPERATION	AVERAGE FREQUENCY PER YEAR	MINUTES PER 1000 SQ. FT.	MATERIAL PER 100 SQ. FT.	AVERAGE EQUIPMENT COSTS
LAWNS				
Mow—16″ hand	30	10		75.00
18″ power	30	5		175.00
25″ power rider	30	3		450.00
58″ power rider	30	1		2200.00
Fertilize - (cyclone) (24″ spreader)	2	3	3.00	35.00
Annual	1	15	3.00/yr.	35.00
3 year (Pax)	1/3	15	4.00/3 yrs.	35.00
Weed Control (2—4—D+)			.20	
3 gal. hand pump	2	15	.20	21.00
Power rig—30″ boom	2	4	.20	350.00
Rake				
Hand (cavex)	1	60		7.50
Power (20″—24″)	1	10		350.00
Sweep				
Leaf rake	3	25		7.50
25″ Sweep rake	3	5		140.00
30″ Power rake	3	2		350.00
Edge & Trim & Clean Up		Minimum 1000 sq. ft.		
Hand (1 wheel mow)				42.00
Walks	30	25		
Shrub edge	10	60		
Gas power (Cooper)				140.00
Walks	30	5		
Shrub edge	10	20		
Vacuum—30″ Gas-outdoors with shrub hose and large wheels	3	Minimum 1000 sq. ft. 5		680.00

PERSONNEL, TIME AND LABOR DEMANDS

AREA AND OPERATION	AVERAGE FREQUENCY PER YEAR	MINUTES PER 1000 SQ. FT.	MATERIAL PER 100 SQ. FT.	AVERAGE EQUIPMENT COSTS
Shrub Areas				
Weed				
Hand hoe	15	60		6.50
Spray out	10	15	.35	21.00
Spray after mulch	5	10	.07	21.00
Police Up				
Hand pick-up	30	15		
Vacuum (gas-outdoors)	30	7		680.00
Prune	5	60		25.00
Fertilize	1	5	1.00	35.00
Mulch				
Ferti mulch	2	30	50.00	
Course sawdust	2	30	15.00	
Spray (pests)	2	30	.50	21.00
Paved Areas				
Walks				
Sweep - hand	30	30		10.00
Vacuum	30	4		680.00
Snow removal	10			
Hand		80		5.00
Power (24")		12		350.00
Drives & Parking				
Vacuum	10	3		680.00
Snow Control	10	10		350.00
Cut strips along curbs, drain, center - and over parking markings lines only				

PERSONNEL, TIME AND LABOR DEMANDS

AREA AND OPERATION	AVERAGE FREQUENCY PER YEAR	MINUTES PER 1000 SQ. FT.	MATERIAL PER 100 SQ. FT.	AVERAGE EQUIPMENT COSTS
Flower Beds				
Spring Prepare	1	200	10.00	
Plant (flats)	1	600	40.00	
Weed - no mulch	25	60		7.50
Cultivate - no mulch	25	30		7.50
Mulch	1	30	50.00	
Weed with mulch no cultivation	15	20		7.50
Spray	3	10	.35	21.00
Fertilize (24:8:16)	2	5	1.50	35.00
Police-Up	30			
Hand pick-up		15		
Vacuum (outside)		10		680.00
Fall Clean-Up Include pick-up mulch for re-use	1	400		584.00
Trees				
Prune				
From ground	2	20		35.00
High work (if needed)	1/4	60		350.00
Fertilize (24:8:16)	1	30	.25	35.00
Pest Control				
Spray	3	20	.35	350.00
Systemic	1	10	.75	5.00

PERSONNEL TIME AND LABOR REQUIREMENTS

MOVING MATERIALS BY WHEELBARROW

(Load, wheel, dump and return)

for 100 ft. will take 4 minutes.
for 200 ft. will take 5 minutes.
for 300 ft. will take 6 minutes.

LEVELING PER CUBIC YARD

| | | Average cu. yds. per eight-hour day using a fifty-minute hour | | |
Ordinary Soil		Tractor *	Hrs. **	2 ***
Plowing and rooting	280-320	8	8	.035
Using 1 sq. yd. Ferguson or scraper	30-40 (depends upon length of haul)	8	8	133
Shoveling and grading by hand	4-6	—	—	.137
Spreading topsoils: mechanical	60-100	8	8	.166

*Machine
**Operator
***Labor hours per cu. yd.

EXCAVATION PER CUBIC YARD

| | | Average cu. yds. per eight-hour day using a fifty-minute hour | | |
Ordinary Soil		Tractor *	Hrs. **	***
Plowing and loosening soil	280-320	8	8	.025
Drag scraper excavation	Move 100' to dump 20-25	8	8	.375
Dig, shovel and load by hand	5-8	—	—	1.375
Trenches 4-5' deep, hand labor	4-5	—	—	1.75
Pits and holes to 6' deep	4	—	—	2.00
Backfill be hand	16-18	—	—	.47
Spread soil or other loose material by hand	40-48	—	—	.18

LAWN WORK
(Figured in sq. ft. per hr. per man)

Light Soil
1 man will finish grade 500 sq. ft. per hr.

Heavy Soil
1 man will finish grade 375 sq. ft. per hr.

Seeding . . . . .4000 sq. ft. per hr.

Fertilizing . . . . .5000 sq. ft. per hr.

Raking Seed . . . . .3000 sq. ft. per hr.

Top Dress . . . . .2500 sq. ft. per hr.

CONSTRUCTION

Digging Trenches

Figure 10 ft. 1' x 1¼' per hr.
Figure 5 ft. 1' x 2 per hr.

Laying Drain Tile

(Clean trench bottom, lay tile, cover with tar paper and gravel; or cement if bell pipe.) Figure 5 ft. per hr.

GRADING OPERATIONS

Loosening soil to 6'' deep

a. Light Soils

Tractor will loosen 2700 sq. ft. per hr.
Rototiller will loosen 1550 sq. ft. per hr.
Hand labor will loosen 63 sq. ft. per hr.

b. Heavy Soils

Tractor will loosen 1900 sq. ft. per hr.
Rototiller will loosen 700 sq. ft. per hr.
Hand labor will loosen 40 sq. ft. per hr.

c. Excavation by Hand

One man can excavate 5 cu. yds. dirt
thrown to one side in 8 hrs.

d. Loading Trucks

One man can load from ground 5 cu. yds.
of loose dirt to truck in 3 hrs.

Grading Loosened Soil

a. Light Soils

Ferguson tractor will grade 1850 sq. ft. per hour.

b. Heavy Soils

Ferguson tractor will grade 1600 sq. ft. per hour.
Hand labor will grade 250 sq. ft. per hr.

Spreading Top Soil (Hand labor)

to 1'' depth 1.16 yds. per man hr.
to 2'' depth 1.5 cu. yds. per man hr.
to 3'' depth 2.0 cu. yds. per man hr.
to 4'' depth 2.5 cu. yds. per man hr.
to 6'' depth 2.3 cu. yds. per man hr.

MONEY MANAGEMENT
CASH FLOW COMPARISONS AS RELATED TO COSTS AND VOLUME

A #of Units	B Total Fixed Costs	C Fixed Costs Each	D Total Product Costs	E Product Cost Each	F Total Costs Each	G Mark Up-% Purchase	H Sale Price Each	I Total Sales	J Total Net Profit	K %Profit Over Costs
100	$500	$5.00	$500	$5.00	$10.00	20%	$11.00	$1100	$100	10.00%
100	$500	$5.00	$500	$5.00	$10.00	60%	$13.00	$1300	$300	30.00%
200	$500	$2.50	$1000	$5.00	$7.50	20%	8.50	$1700	$200	13.3 %
200	$500	$2.50	$1000	$5.00	$7.50	60%	$10.50	$2100	$600	40.00%
1000	$500	$0.50	$5000	$5.00	$5.50	20%	$ 6.50	$6500	$1000	18.18%
1000	$500	$0.50	$5000	$5.00	$5.50	60%	$ 8.50	$8500	$3000	54.54%

If we buy 1000 and sell at 100 rate price and remain competitive:

A	B	C	D	E	F	G	H	I	J	K
1000	$500	$0.50	$5000	$5.00	$5.50	—	$11.00	$11,000	$6000	109.00%
1000	$500	$0.50	$5000	$5.00	$5.50	—	$13.00	$13,000	$8000	145.00%

If we add another employee which adds $50 to fixed costs:

A	B	C	D	E	F	G	H	I	J	K
100	$550	$5.50	$500	$5.00	$10.50	20%	$11.50	$1150	$100	09.5 %
100	$550	$5.50	$500	$5.00	$10.50	60%	$13.50	$1350	$300	28.00%
200	$550	$2.75	$1000	$5.00	$ 7.50	20%	$ 8.75	$1750	$200	12.9 %
200	$550	$2.75	$1000	$5.00	$ 7.75	60%	$10.75	$2150	$600	38.7 %
1000	$550	$0.55	$5000	$5.00	$ 5.55	20%	$ 6.55	$6550	$1000	18.00%
1000	$550	$0.55	$5000	$5.00	$ 5.55	60%	$ 8.55	$8550	$3000	54.4 %

If we buy only 100 and have to sell at the 1000 rate to be competitive:

A	B	C	D	E	F	G	H	I	J	K
100	$550	$5.50	$500	$5.00	$10.50	—	$ 6.55	$ 655	($395)	62.4 %

Note: we did not figure in discounts, etc, for simplicity sake.

A. These can be items sold, units of service or other units of products delivered.

B. Includes that portion of all operating costs attributable to these items: both production and support labor, rent, taxes, insurance and other items not sold as a part of that item. Basically these are the costs which are fixed and remain the same whether you sell or use ten, thirty or a hundred units. These are the underlying costs attendant to being in business.

C.   B divided by A

D.   A times E

E.   Total cost of products or services as costed to that item: if it is a product, it is the cost of purchase, shipping, taxes, etc. If it is a serivce, this includes labor and materials expended directly for a client on a site. It is essential to make certain that all product related costs are listed either in "C" or "E".

F.   C plus E

G.   That percentage used as a mark-up

H.   That percentage times E plus C plus E

I.   Equals A times H

J.   Equals I minus B minus D

K.   Equals percentage J is of B plus D

THE APPROXIMATE NUMBER OF SEEDS
PER POUND AND NORMAL SEEDING RATES FOR
TURF GRASS SPECIES

Turfgrass species	Approximate number of seeds per lb.	Normal seeding rates	
		lb per 1000 sq. ft.	Number of seeds per sq. in.
Bahiagrass	166,000	6-8	7-9
Bentgrass:			
colonial	8,723,000	0.5-1	30-60
creeping	7,890,000	0.5-1	27-55
velvet	11,800.000	0.5-1	41-81
Bermudagrass, hulled	1,787,000	1-1.5	12-19
Bluegrass:			
Canada	2,495,000	1-1.5	17-26
Kentucky	2,177,000	1-1.5	15-23
rough	2,540,000	1-1.5	18-26
Buffalograss	50,000	3-6	1-2
Carpetgrass	1,123,000	1.5-2.5	12-19
Centipedegrass	400,000	4-6	11-17
Fescue:			
chewings	546,000	3.5-4.5	13-17
meadow	227,000	7-9	11-14
red	546,000	3.5-4.5	13-17
sheep	530,000	3.5-4.5	13-16
tall	227,000	7-9	11-14
Grama, blue	898,000	1.5-2.5	9-16
Redtop	4,990,000	0.5-1	17-34
Ryegrass:			
Italian	227,000	7-9	11-14
perennial	227,000	7-9	11-14
Timothy	1,134,000	1-2	8-16
Wheatgrass, fairway	324,000	3-5	7-11
Zoysiagrass	1,369,000	2-3	19-28

THE DEMYSTIFYING OF PERCENTAGES

To compute percentage, use the formula

$$\frac{P \times O}{100} = T \quad \text{or} \quad P \times O = 100\ T$$

P = %
O = Original Quantity
T = Total or that quantity which is the P (%) part of Quantity O.

Samples:

1. 23 is what part of 80?   P = ?   O = 80   T = 23
    P × O = 100   T = 80   P = 2300
    P = 28.75

2. 15% of 67 = ?   P = 15   O = 67   T = ?
    P × O = 100   T = 15 × 67 = 100   T = 1005 = 100 T
    T = 10.05

3. 29 is 32% of ?   P = 32   O = ?   T = 29
    P × O = 100   T = 32   O = 2900
    O = 90.625

INTEREST AND THE COST OF MONEY

Approximate Costs to Pay off In One (1) Year:

	0% Interest		8% Interest		9¾ Interest		12% Interest	
Cash Needed	Cost/ Month	Total Repay	Cost/ Month	Total Repay	Cost/ Month	Total Repay	Cost/ Month	Total Repay
1,000	83.33	1,000	86.99	1,043.88	87.80	1,053.60	88.85	1,066.19
10,000	833.33	10,000	869.89	10,438.68	878.00	10,536.00	888.49	10,661.88
100,000	8333.33	100,000	8698.90	104,386.80	8780.00	105,360.00	8884.90	106,618.80

Approximate Cost to Pay Off in Ten (10) Years:

1,000	8.33	1,000	12.13	1,455.99	13.08	1,569.36	14.35	1,721.76
10,000	83.33	10,000	121.33	14,559.96	130.78	15,693.60	143.48	17,217.60
100,000	833.33	100,000	1213.33	145,599.60	1307.80	156,936.00	1434.80	172,176.00

Approximate Cost to Pay Off In Twenty (20) Years:

1,000	4.17	1,000	8.37	2,007.60	9.49	2,276.64	11.01	2,642.64
10,000	41.67	10,000	83.65	20,076.00	94.86	22,766.40	110.11	26,426.40
100,000	416.66	100,000	836.50	200,760.00	948.60	227,664.00	1101.10	264,264.00

General Conditions

All areas, structures, features, etc., shall be provided with full and ready access for standard construction, maintenance, and operations and equipment. Adequate storage will be designed and provided for service and operations, equipment, tools, material, etc.

Basic Grades	% Grade		Ratio
Maximum Unsupported Cut	100	%	(1.1)
Maximum Unsupported Full	50	%	(2.1)
Maximum Simple Construction	33 1/3	%	(3.1)
Maximum Practical Landscape	30	%	
Maximum Lawn Slope	20	%	(5.1)
Maximum Walk Ramp	15	%	
Maximum Drive Slope	12	%	
Maximum Slope for Black Top Drive	10	%	(10.1)
Maximum Fast Highway or Dirt Road. also Optimum Drain Slope From Building	5	%	(20.1)
Maximum Freeway, Also Minimum for Slope From Building	3	%	
Optimum Playfields, Paved or Other Exterior "Flat" Areas	2	%	(50.1)
Minimum Landscape or Paved Surface	1	%	(100.1)

Landscaping for Parking

Landscape plantings shall be provided for all parking areas.

Minimum—1 tree for every 15 cars.

Maximum unplanted areas—150 feet radius from each and every spot in parking to a landscaped area with a minimum of 1.0 percent of total parking use area to be in landscape plantings.

Median Strip planting—minimum of 8 feet wide. If median strips are to be walked across, trees planted in mineral chip (slag, gravel, etc.) are suggested. Trees used shall be of a type to permit pruning up to give full 7-foot high clearance of curb side. No lawn grass shall be used in parking median strips.

Landscaping for Parking (continued)

Drives

	Minimum	Optimum
One Way	9'	12'
Two Way	20'	26'

Drive curves minimum inside radius for cars shall be 18 feet; for large trucks, 32 feet, for specialty equipment, get data from manufacturer. For large vehicles, add to road width on curves to compensate for vehicle length. For all vehicles, provide full sight clearance and adequate vehicle overhang clearance (up to 8 feet).

Curb Cuts (drive entry and/or exits)

One Way	18' at narrow point
Two Way	30' at narrow point

The maximum grade is 8 percent, optimum not over 3 percent. Avoid sharp grade changes, gutters, dips, etc. Consider using road side acceleration and deceleration lanes where possible.

Walks

	Minimum Width	Optimum Width
Main Walks	72'	on up
Secondary	48'	60'
Others	36'	58'

Walks at intersections shall be provided with "corner fills" with a minimum of 6 feet radius. Maximum slope for walk ramps is 15 percent. Consider using steps when grading exceeds 6 percent.

Steps

Exterior steps shall be provided with cheek or shoulder ramps. Top grade of ramp—1 inch above sod or soil level.

Maximum slope	6" riser, 12" tread
Optimum slope	5½" riser, 15" tread
Minimum slope	3" riser, 24" tread
	Less than that, consider use of ramped walks

NOTE: Provide ramp access to all buildings for handicapped.
Maximum 1:6 slope

Lawn Areas

Lawn shall be used only where fully accessible and comfortably maintainable, with full normal access for irrigation, mowing, fertilizing, etc. Lawn areas shall be designed open and clutter free. As far as practical, shrub and ground cover areas shall be separated from lawn areas by a concrete mow strip (4 inches deep by 6 inches wide) or 1-inch by 6-inch redwood headers or appropriate steel curb, their tops being placed flush with sod soil level. Angle corners shall be avoided. Edges at corners shall be curved.

Exterior steps shall be provided with cheek or shoulder ramps. Top grade of ramp—1 inch above sod or soil level.

Maximum slope   6″ riser, 12″ tread
Optimum slope   5½″ riser, 15″ tread
Minimum slope   3″ riser, 24″ tread
                 Less than that, consider use
                 of ramped walks
NOTE: Provide ramp access to all buildings for handicapped.
        Maximum 1:6 slope

Lawn Area Size	Minimum Radius Inside Curve	Minimum Radius Outside Curve
Under 10,000 sq. ft.	6 ft.	2 ft.
10,000 - 20,000 sq. ft.	10 ft.	4 ft.
20,000 - 130,000 sq. ft.	12 ft.	6 ft.
Over 130,000 sq. ft.	20 ft.	12 ft.

Lawn grass shall not be used in any planting strip less than 36 inches wide unless as an extension of a continuous larger area.

Planned lawn areas shall, if necessary, be modified with retaining walls, cuts, fills or others as needed to meet Basic Grades as listed.

Where traffic lanes do develop in spite of adequate, proper culture, stepping stones, walks or other measures will be taken to accept the wear and compaction.

Adequate and appropriate irrigation systems will be provided.

Only grass types proven fully adaptable for that area and soil will be used.

Lawn Areas (continued)

Lawn grass shall not be used in any planting strip less than 36 inches wide unless as an extension of a continuous larger area.

Planned lawn areas shall, if necessary, be modified with retaining walls, cuts, fills or others as needed to meet Basic Grades as listed.

Where traffic lanes do develop in spite of adequate, proper culture, stepping stones, walks or other measures will be taken to accept the wear and comapction.

Adequate and appropriate irrigation systems will be provided.

Only grass types proven fully adaptable for that area and soil will be used.

Shrub Areas

Minimum width	18″
Maximum width	10′ from an exposed side
Minimum grade	1% slope
Maximum grade	20% slope

Planter Beds
(flowers excluding display floral bed—here no size restriction)

Minimum width	6″
Maximum width	36″ from exposed side
Minimum grade	5% slope
Maximum grade	20% slope

Planter Boxes

	Minimum	Maximum
Width	12″	36″ from exposed side
Length	18″	no maximum
Depth	24″	no maximum

Drain holes shall be provided no less than every two feet of perimeter at base of sides to insure drainage. Holes shall be no less than one-inch in size and no further than one-quarter inch from bottom with the bottom flat or sloped toward the holes. One-half inch of washed pea gravel shall be placed at bottom of the planter. This shall be overlaid with a 1-inch blanket of fine glass wool (unwrapped, auch as P.P.G. Super-Fine glass Insulation Batting). Above this soil shall be added a homogenous, unstratified planter mix of good drainage.

Tree Plantings

Trees shall be planted in shrub areas wherever practical. Where trees must be planted in lawn areas, trees must be planted at least 8 feet (at center) away from any shrub planting, wall, fence or other obstruction that will hinder free lawn mower movement.

Deciduous trees shall be planted no closer than 8 feet from any walk or drive. Evergreen trees shall be planted no closer than 2 feet greater than expected mature radius of branching, unless tree is to be espaliered.

Lawn trees shall be provided with 24 inches of bare, sod free, sandy soil beyond and around a full circle of the tree. The soil shall be no lower than one-half inch below sod soil grade (sand panning) for easier mowing.

Gross Tree Populations

Clumps—Close plantings where individual tree stems are no further than 5 feet apart at center, treat as individual trees.

Groves—Close plantings of 3 or more trees with 5 or more feet in between two or more individual trees in planting. Ground surface to be covered with mulch only, such as bark, sand, gravel, wood chips, etc. No plantings or undergrowth kept. Maximum 1 tree per 100 square feet.

Groupings—Tree groups planned with planted undergrowth other than grass or turf. Maximum 1 tree per 600 square feet.

Lawn Trees—Those planted in or adjacent to lawn areas. Where tree will at reasonable maturity extend at least one-third of its top or branch growth over to shade a lawn area. If planted in the lawn, tree shall be "sand panned." If planted in shrub area, tree shall be at least 6 feet from lawn edge. Maximum 1 lawn tree per 2,000 square feet. Optimum for lawn care not to exceed an overall average 1 tree per 10,000 square feet of lawn, not figuring into total open planned playfields.

Mulches

All "non-turf" ground or soil surface areas shall be mulches except in rough or undeveloped areas. Here, mulching is optional.

Ground cover (herbaceous) plantings shall receive at least 1 inch of mulch at planting time. Spaces between plants shall have this mulch maintained during fill-in growing time.

Areas planted to woody plants shall be provided with no less than 2 inches of mulch. This shall be maintained as a soil protection and weed control measure.

Where ground has over a 6 percent slope, soil will be contour terraced before mulch is applied to even further improve erosion control.

Preferred mulches are:

Sand—Usually for herbaceous plants, to provide soft texture.

Slag Chips—High density, sharp edges, one-quarter inch to five eighths inch diameter for flat to gentle ground, especially where walk-through traffic is expected, these hold position very well.

Mulches (continued)

Pea Gravel— If walk-through traffic is expected, provide walk or stepping stones, pea gravel tends to scatter easily.

Processed Wood Products—Bark, etc. Use primarily those in the one-sixteenth inch to 1 inch range (larger chunks are more for ornamentation). If the larger pieces are used, increase depth of mulch to 3 times the diameter of the largest pieces. These are expensive but help build soil.

Rough Cut Wood and Pruning Chips—As derived from regular tree removal chipping operations. This mulch is not quite as attractive as processed wood, but much cheaper and holds position better.

Each type has its place, but slag chips and rough cut wood chips prove more desirable in most cases.

Irrigation

All planting areas shall be provided with adequate "on site" water sources. Sprinklers shall be designed to provide uniform, even coverage at a rate not to exceed 1 inch of water per hour. Separate valving shall be provided for variations in demand such as shady areas and full sun areas, slopes over 6 percent and flat areas, shrubs and turf and flower beds. Manual valving should be considered for problem situations. In fact, in most situations, if systems are designed with low enough application rates to meet soil types, manual systems may be preferred.

Maximum Precipitation Rates

Light Soil — 1" per hour or less
Medium Soil — 1/2" per hour or less
Heavy Soil — 1/3" per hour or less

Large enough piping sizes shall be provided to supply full water use, not only for irrigation but cleaning, etc.

Suggested Minimum Water Lines for Landscape Use
(not including culinary and fire control)

3,000 sq. ft. or under	¾" pipe
3,000 — 5,000 sq. ft.	1 " pipe
5,000 — 10,000 sq. ft.	1½" pipe
10,000 — 15,000 sq. ft.	2 " pipe
15,000 — 1 acre	2½" pipe

Hose bibs or quick coupler valves shall be provided a minimum of every 100 feet where paved areas are maintained (walks, steps, patios, etc.); where heated structures are involved, frost-free bibs shall be provided from and for building exterior services. All open area bibs and valves will be contained for safe and convenient use and operations.

Plant Materials

All plant materials used shall be of types proven hardy for the area and situation. New, novel, or "different" plants shall be restricted to a bare minimum. All plants shall be healthy, true to name, and up to a full size specified.

Trees shall be sturdy enough to stand under rain and wind without stakes with the caliper of stem adequate for the head it is to carry. It should, if bare root, have an adequate root system.

Minimum Deciduous Tree Relation Guide:

Tree Height	Minimum Caliper	Minimum Root Spread
5	¾ ''	12''
6	1 ''	14''
7	1 ''	16''
8	1¼ ''	18''
9	1½ ''	20''
10	1¾ ''	24''
12	2 ''	28''
14	3 ''	32''
16	4 ''	38''
18	6 ''	42''

Other Environmental Concerns

Design to reduce motor traffic and expedite foot traffic.

Provide adequate storage and access for service operations and maintenance equipment and needs.

Provide adequate but minimum outdoor lighting. To reduce energy consumption, use only high efficiency units.

Insist that all sprays, pesticides, and other hazardous materials be available to and used only by those properly instructed and qualified.

DESIGN STANDARDS FOR POSTS
AND OTHER PHYSICAL OBSTRUCTIONS

1. Strips of ground between parallel curb strips and between walk and curb strips next to parking areas where cars hang over shall not be planted to lawn, shrubs, or any other ground cover but shall be paved or surfaced with an organic or inorganic chip mulch as a ground cover.

Trees or posts may be placed in these areas but must be so located as to not sustain damage from normal parking operations.

2. Any posts, poles, stands, etc., placed in lawn areas shall meet at least the following minimum:

Single isolated post shall be provided with no less than a 6-inch radius (beyond post radius) paved mow strip or apron. This is to be at soil level.

Where two or more posts are joined by an overhead sign that blocks through passage of riding mower or where posts are closer than 8 feet apart, the area under and between posts shall be shaped to permit convenient mowing and shall be surfaced with an appropriate organic or inorganic mulch or shall be planted to a low type evergreen shrub such as tamarix juniper, with a chip or bark mulch cover on soil. If extensive, pave areas unclear.

3. Posts or obstructions placed within 2 feet 4 inches of a curb, building, or other obstruction shall have plantings installed or have a mow strip and apron placed to eliminate grass between post and curb or obstruction all designed to accommodate riding power mowing equipment, when possible.

4. Posts or plantings placed between 2 feet and 8 feet from curbs, buildings, or other obstructions which have unmowable area under and between, shall be surfaced with inorganic chip mulch or planted and mulched.

5. Where tree planting populations and/or other obstructions prohibit normal economical mowing practices, "under planting," mulch surfacing, or both shall be provided on the unmowable areas.

6. Lawn strips less than 30 inches wide shall be optional with maintenance staff as to replacement with shrubs or mulch.

7. Walk intersection corners shall be rounded where traffic dictates with a minimum inside radius of 6 feet and up, to include worn areas.

8. Inlaid stepping stones may be used where "spot wearing" is involved.

9. Convenient trash collection locations shall be established and dressed.

10. Where definite foot traffic lanes develop in spite of normal efforts to prevent, walks will be put in. Temporary "black top" surfacing being permitted where funds cannot be readily obtained for concrete.

Live Plant Areas: 200 sq. ft. of live plant area per person involved on site to include one tree for every two people, plus one tree for every car in use. At least every 5th tree should be an evergreen tree — (people areas, not parking areas - for parking areas one tree per 15 cars.)

Minimums for Surfaced Areas . . . .   25 sq. ft. minimum per person - passive
50 sq. ft. minimum per person - semiactive
600 sq. ft. per person - very active -(skiing, etc.)

Play Lots - Age one to seven - Fenced . . . .   100 sq. ft. minimum plus 50 sq. ft. per child. Maximum 100 children per lot.

Play area - Age seven to fourteen -
      (8 or more children) . . . .   2400 sq. ft. open area plus 50 sq. ft. per person.

Game area adults - (8 or more people) . . . .   3600 sq. ft. open area plus 50 sq. ft. per person.

48

LABOR ESTIMATING
Example of how to estimate cost differences between
doing a job mechanically as opposed to by hand.

Hand Sweep Cost
  734 hours x 2.5 . . . . = 1,835 x \$4.45/hr. . . . . = \$8,161.75 per annum

Power Sweep cost
  183 hours x 2.5 . . . .= 457.5 x \$4.55/hr. . . . . = \$2,081.63 per annum

Gross savings . . . . = \$6,084.12 per annum

Depreciation—\$8,500 (10 years) . . . . = \$ 850.00 per annum

Operating Costs—gas, oil, repairs . . . . = \$2,400.00 per annum

* Estimated Net Savings . . . . = \$2,834.12 per annum

* Return on Investment . . . . = 33.34 % or 2.9 years

*Example here is comparing costs between hand and power sweeping of paving areas,
but the form could be used on almost any type of landscape work.

SOIL
EXCAVATION
AND
BACKFILL

TREE BALL SIZES—WEIGHTS, ETC.

Diameter	Depth	Area in Sq. Feet	Cubic Feet	Weight in Lbs.	Diameter	Depth	Area in Sq. Feet	Cubic Feet	Weight in Lbs.
8''	6''	0.35	0.15	13	27''	12''	3.98	3.49	297
8''	8''	''	0.21	18	27''	15''	''	4.36	370
10''	6''	0.54	0.24	21	27''	18''	''	5.23	444
10''	8''	''	0.32	28	27''	20''	''	5.81	491
10''	10''	''	0.39	34	27''	22''	''	6.39	532
12''	6''	0.78	0.34	29	27''	24''	''	6.97	588
12''	9''	''	0.52	45	28''	14''	4.28	4.36	370
12''	12''	''	0.68	58	28''	16''	''	4.99	424
14''	6''	1.08	0.47	40	28''	18''	''	5.62	477
14''	8''	''	0.63	53	28''	20''	''	6.24	530
14''	10''	''	0.78	66	28''	22''	''	6.87	583
14''	12''	''	0.94	80	28''	24''	''	7.49	637
14''	14''	''	1.10	94	30''	15''	4.91	5.37	456
15''	8''	1.23	0.72	62	30''	18''	''	6.44	547
15''	10''	''	0.90	76	30''	21''	''	7.51	638
15''	12''	''	1.07	91	30''	24''	''	8.58	729
15''	14''	''	1.26	107	30''	27''	''	9.65	820
15''	15''	''	1.35	115	33''	15''	5.94	6.50	552
16''	10''	1.40	1.13	96	33''	18''	''	7.80	663
16''	12''	''	1.21	103	33''	21''	''	9.10	773
16''	14''	''	1.42	120	33''	24''	''	10.40	884
16''	15''	''	1.52	129	33''	27''	''	11.69	994
18''	12''	1.77	1.54	131	36''	18''	7.07	9.27	788
18''	14''	''	1.81	155	36''	21''	''	10.83	920
18''	16''	''	2.05	175	36''	24''	''	12.37	1,052
20''	12''	2.18	1.91	163	36''	27''	''	13.91	1,183
20''	14''	''	2.24	191	36''	30''	''	15.46	1,314
20''	15''	''	2.39	203	39''	18''	8.30	10.77	916
20''	16''	''	2.54	216	39''	21''	''	12.69	1,079
20''	18''	''	2.87	244	39''	24''	''	14.52	1,129
21''	12''	2.40	2.10	178	39''	27''	''	16.35	1,270
21''	15''	''	2.63	224	39''	30''	''	18.15	1,411
21''	18''	''	3.15	268	39''	33''	''	19.97	1,550
21''	20''	''	3.50	298	40''	18''	8.73	11.46	974
22''	12''	2.64	2.31	196	40''	21''	''	13.38	1,137
22''	15''	''	2.89	246	40''	24''	''	15.29	1,300
22''	16''	''	3.08	262	40''	27''	''	17.19	1,461
22''	18''	''	3.46	294	40''	30''	''	19.10	1,623
22''	21''	''	4.04	343	40''	33''	''	21.00	1,785
24''	12''	3.14	2.74	233	40''	36''	''	22.92	1,948
24''	15''	''	3.44	292	42''	18''	9.62	12.63	1,074
24''	16''	''	3.65	310	42''	21''	''	14.74	1,253
24''	18''	''	4.13	351	42''	24''	''	16.85	1,432
24''	21''	''	4.80	408	42''	27''	''	18.95	1,610
26''	12''	3.69	3.23	275	42''	30''	''	21.05	1,789
26''	14''	''	3.77	320	42''	33''	''	23.15	1,970
26''	15''	''	4.03	343	42''	36''	''	25.25	2,146
26''	16''	''	4.30	365					
26''	18''	''	4.83	411					
26''	20''	''	5.37	457					
26''	21''	''	5.64	480					

SOIL EXCAVATION AND BACKFILL

TREE BALL SIZES—WEIGHTS, ETC.

Diameter	Depth	Area in Sq. Feet	Cubic Feet	Weight in Lbs.	Diameter	Depth	Area in Sq. Feet	Cubic Feet	Weight in Lbs.
45"	18"	11.05	14.51	1,234	60"	33"	19.64	47.26	4,017
45"	21"	"	16.93	1,439	60"	36"	"	51.56	4,383
45"	24"	"	19.35	1,644	60"	39"	"	55.86	4,748
45"	27"	"	21.77	1,849	60"	42"	"	60.15	5,113
45"	30"	"	24.18	2,054	66"	21"	23.75	36.38	3,092
45"	33"	"	26.59	2,260	66"	24"	"	41.56	3,533
45"	36"	"	29.00	2,465	66"	27"	"	46.75	3,974
48"	21"	12.57	19.24	1,635	66"	30"	"	51.96	4,417
48"	24"	"	22.00	1,870	66"	33"	"	57.15	4,858
48"	27"	"	24.75	2,104	66"	36"	"	62.34	5,299
48"	30"	"	27.50	2,337	66"	39"	"	67.54	5,741
48"	33"	"	30.25	2,571	66"	42"	"	72.74	6,183
48"	36"	"	33.00	2,804	72"	24"	28.28	49.49	4,207
48"	39"	"	35.75	3,038	72"	27"	"	55.67	4,732
50"	21"	13.64	20.89	1,776	72"	30"	"	61.85	5,257
50"	24"	"	23.87	2,029	72"	33"	"	68.04	5,784
50"	27"	"	26.86	2,283	72"	36"	"	74.23	6,310
50"	30"	"	29.84	2,536	72"	39"	"	80.42	6,836
50"	33"	"	32.82	2,790	72"	42"	"	86.62	7,363
50"	36"	"	35.80	3,043	78"	24"	33.18	58.06	4,935
50"	39"	"	38.79	3,296	78"	27"	"	65.32	5,552
50"	42"	"	41.78	3,550	78"	30"	"	72.58	6,170
51"	21"	14.18	21.72	1,846	78"	33"	"	79.84	6,786
51"	24"	"	24.82	2,110	78"	36"	"	87.11	7,404
51"	27"	"	27.92	2,373	78"	39"	"	94.36	8,021
51"	30"	"	31.02	2,637	78"	42"	"	101.61	8,637
51"	33"	"	34.12	2,900	78"	45"	"	108.86	9,253
51"	36"	"	37.22	3,163	78"	48"	"	116.11	9,879
51"	39"	"	40.33	3,428	84"	24"	38.49	67.36	5,725
51"	42"	"	43.43	3,692	84"	27"	"	75.78	6,441
54"	21"	15.91	24.36	2,071	84"	30"	"	84.20	7,157
54"	24"	"	27.84	2,367	84"	33"	"	92.62	7,873
54"	27"	"	31.32	2,663	84"	36"	"	101.04	8,588
54"	30"	"	34.80	2,959	84"	39"	"	109.46	9,304
54"	33"	"	38.28	3,255	84"	42"	"	117.88	10,020
54"	36"	"	41.76	3,559	84"	45"	"	126.30	10,736
54"	39"	"	45.24	3,846	84"	48"	"	134.72	11,451
54"	42"	"	48.73	4,142	90"	24"	44.18	77.32	6,572
57"	21"	17.71	27.11	2,305	90"	27"	"	86.98	7,393
57"	24"	"	31.00	2,635	90"	30"	"	96.64	8,214
57"	27"	"	34.88	2,965	90"	33"	"	106.30	9,036
57"	30"	"	38.76	3,294	90"	36"	"	115.96	9,857
57"	33"	"	42.63	3,623	90"	39"	"	125.63	10,679
57"	36"	"	46.50	3,952	90"	42"	"	135.30	11,500
57"	39"	"	50.37	4,281	90"	45"	"	144.97	12,323
57"	42"	"	54.24	4,610	90"	48"	"	154.63	13,144
60"	21"	19.64	30.07	2,556	96"	30"	50.27	109.96	9,347
60"	24"	"	34.37	2,921	96"	33"	"	120.96	10,282
60"	27"	"	38.67	3,286	96"	36"	"	131.96	11,217
60"	30"	"	42.96	3,652	96"	39"	"	142.96	12,152

HEDGE TRENCHES–PER LINEAL FEET
CUBIC MEASURE FOR EXCAVATION

												Width											
	1'	1¼'	1½'	1¾'	2'	2¼'	2½'	2¾'	3'	3¼'	3½'	3¾'	4'	4¼'	4½'	4¾'	5'	5½'	6'	7'	8'	9'	10'
Depth																							
1'	1.20	1.50	1.80	2.10	2.40	2.70	3.00	3.30	3.60	3.90	4.20	4.50	4.80	5.10	5.40	5.70	6.00	6.60	7.20	8.40	9.60	10.8	12.0
1¼'	1.50	1.88	2.25	2.63	3.00	3.37	3.75	4.13	4.50	4.88	5.25	5.63	6.00	6.37	6.75	7.12	7.50	8.25	9.00	10.5	12.0	13.5	15.0
1½'	1.80	2.25	2.70	3.15	3.60	4.05	4.50	4.95	5.40	5.85	6.30	6.75	7.20	7.65	8.10	8.55	9.00	9.90	10.8	12.6	14.4	16.2	18.0
1¾'	2.10	2.63	3.15	3.68	4.20	4.73	5.25	5.78	6.30	6.83	7.35	7.88	8.40	8.93	9.45	9.98	10.5	11.6	12.6	14.7	16.8	19.9	21.0
2'	2.40	3.00	3.60	4.20	4.80	5.40	6.00	6.60	7.20	7.80	8.40	9.00	9.60	10.2	10.8	11.4	12.0	13.2	14.4	16.8	19.2	21.6	24.0
2¼'	2.70	3.38	4.05	4.73	5.40	6.08	6.75	7.43	8.10	8.7C	9.45	10.1	10.8	11.5	12.2	12.8	13.5	14.9	16.2	19.9	21.6	24.4	27.0
2½'	3.00	3.75	4.50	5.25	6.00	6.75	7.50	8.25	9.00	9.75	10.5	11.3	12.0	12.8	13.5	14.3	15.0	16.5	18.0	21.0	24.0	27.0	30.0
2¾'	3.30	4.13	4.95	5.78	6.60	7.43	8.25	9.08	9.90	10.7	11.6	12.4	13.2	14.0	14.9	15.7	16.5	18.1	19.8	23.1	26.4	29.8	33.0
3'	3.60	4.50	5.40	6.30	7.20	8.10	9.00	9.90	10.8	11.7	12.6	13.5	14.4	15.3	16.2	17.1	18.0	19.8	21.6	25.2	28.8	32.4	36.0
3¼'	3.90	4.88	5.85	6.83	7.80	8.78	9.75	10.7	11.7	12.7	13.7	14.6	15.6	16.6	17.5	18.5	19.5	21.5	23.4	27.3	31.2	35.0	39.0
3½'	4.20	5.25	6.30	7.35	8.40	9.45	10.5	11.6	12.6	13.7	14.7	15.7	16.8	17.8	18.9	20.0	21.0	23.1	25.2	29.4	33.6	37.8	42.0
3¾'	4.50	5.63	6.75	7.88	9.00	10.1	11.3	12.4	13.5	14.7	15.8	16.9	18.0	19.1	20.2	21.3	22.5	24.7	27.0	31.5	36.0	40.4	45.0
4'	4.80	6.00	7.20	8.40	9.60	10.8	12.0	13.2	14.4	15.6	16.8	18.0	19.2	20.4	21.6	22.8	24.0	26.4	28.8	33.6	38.4	43.2	48.0
4¼'	5.10	6.38	7.65	8.93	10.2	11.5	12.8	14.0	15.3	16.6	17.8	19.1	20.4	21.7	23.0	24.2	25.5	28.0	30.6	35.7	40.8	46.0	51.0
4½'	5.40	6.75	8.10	9.45	10.8	12.2	13.5	14.8	16.2	17.6	18.9	20.3	21.6	23.0	24.3	25.6	27.0	29.7	32.4	37.8	43.2	48.6	54.0
4¾'	5.70	7.13	8.55	9.98	11.4	12.8	14.3	15.7	17.1	18.5	20.0	21.3	22.8	24.2	25.7	27.1	28.5	31.4	34.2	40.0	45.6	51.4	57.0
5'	6.00	7.50	9.00	10.5	12.0	13.5	15.0	16.5	18.0	19.5	21.0	22.5	24.0	25.5	27.0	28.5	30.0	33.0	36.0	42.0	48.0	54.0	60.0
5½'	6.60	8.25	9.90	11.6	13.2	14.9	16.5	18.2	19.8	21.5	23.1	24.7	26.4	28.0	29.6	31.4	33.0	36.3	39.6	46.2	52.8	59.2	66.0
6'	7.20	9.00	10.8	12.6	14.4	16.2	18.0	19.8	21.6	23.4	25.2	27.0	28.8	30.6	32.4	34.2	36.0	39.6	43.2	50.4	57.6	64.8	72.0

The above quantities are cubic feet.

SET NO. III - HEDGE TRENCHES

This Chart gives the amount of Excavation in digging trenches of any length from 1' to 10' wide, and 1' to 6' deep.

To operate this chart, take the length of the trench, multiply by the amount shown for the width and depth specified.

Example:

Trench 100' long by 3' wide by 2' deep
3' x 2' = 6.00 cu. ft. plus 20% = 7.20
100 x 7.20 = 720 cu. ft. or 26.7 cu. yds.

From the total cubic contents deduct the ball displacement as shown in Set. No. II to arrive at the amount of top soil required.

Example

Assume that in the above example 34 Hemlocks 5-6' are planted on 3' centers with ball 21" by 15" deep.

Set No. II gives the ball displacement at 2.63 cubic feet per tree.

34 x 2.63 = 89.4 cu. ft. or 3.4 cu. yds.
3.4 cu. yds. deducted from 26.7 = 23.3 cu. yds. top soil required.

SAFE LIMIT RESTRICTIONS (GENERAL GUIDE)

Percent Grade	Restriction Guide
100% (1:1)	Maximum cut slope.
50% (2:1)	Maximum fill slope.
33 1/3% (3:1)	Maximum for simple construction.
30%	Maximum for practical landscape care, use retaining walls where practical.
20%	Maximum lawn slope.
15%	Consider ground cover or shrubs to replace lawn.
12%	Maximum driveway slope.
10%	Steep grade—maximum where snow or ice.
5% (20:1)	Maximum for dirt roads and highways traffic. Optimum drain slope from buildings.
3%	Maximum freeway slope (rolling).
2%	Optimum for playfields—other flat landscapes.
1% (100:1)	Minimum landscape slope.

EXCAVATION AND TOP SOIL—LAWN AREAS

To find the amount of excavation and/or top soil for lawn areas, multiply the area by the number of inches of depth required and divide by 10. This will give the number of cubic feet required. Divide the answer by 27 to find the number of cubic yards. This manner of figuring will include 20% for expansion or shrinkage.

EXAMPLES

Area is 6,432 square feet; Depth is 3 inches
6,432 x 3 = 19,296 ÷ 10 = 1,929.6 cubic feet or 71.5 cubic yards

Area is 288,645 square feet; Depth is 7 inches
288,645 x 7 = 2,020,515 ÷ 10 = 202,051.5 cubic feet or 7,843.4 cubic yards

Area is 11,988 square feet; Depth is 3 feet
11,988 x 36 = 431,568 ÷ 10 = 43,156.8 cubic feet or 1,598.4 cubic yards

Earth expands 20% when loosened up. Top soil shrinks 20% when compacted. Thus these figures for lawns can be used for either excavation or top soil as the 20% is included either way.

Depth Per 1,000 Square Feet	Number Cubic Yards Required
1 inch	3½
4 inches	13
6 inches	21

Depth Per Acre	Number Cubic Yards Required
1 inch	143
4 inches	575
6 inches	858

NURSERY CONTAINER STOCK
Volume of Excavated Soil Resulting From Multiple Plantings
Round Planting Pits

Container Stock	Excavation Yardage* per:		
	10 Plants	100 Plants	1,000 Plants
1 Gallon	0.29	2.9	29.0
5 Gallon	1.33	13.3	133.3
15 Gallon	4.10	41.0	410.0
16" Box	4.67	46.7	467.0
20" Box	5.21	52.1	521.0
24" Box	6.44	64.4	644.0
30" Box	11.33	113.33	1,133.3
36" Box	19.40	194.0	1,940.0
42" Box	24.90	249.0	2,490.0
48" Box	38.70	387.0	3,870.0
54" Box	49.00	490.0	4,900.0
60" Box	70.66	706.6	7,066.0

*Swellage Factor not applied. See Table for swellage of various soils.

NURSERY CONTAINER STOCK
Approximate Back-Fill Volume For Various Container Stock
Round Plant-Pits/Vertical Sides

	Plant Pit Volume in Cubic Feet		Container Stock Displacement in Cubic Feet		Back-Fill Necessary*	
					Cubic Feet	Cubic Yards
(1 gal.)	0.78	(minus)	0.15	(equals)	0.63	.02
(5 gal.)	3.60	—	0.60	=	3.00	.11
(15 gal.)	11.10	—	2.00	=	9.10	.34
(16" Box)	12.60	—	2.50	=	9.35	.35
(20" Box)	14.10	—	4.75	=	10.10	.37
(24" Box)	17.40	—	6.70	=	10.70	.40
(30" Box)	30.60	—	13.60	=	17.00	.63
(36" Box)	52.36	—	23.40	=	28.96	1.07
(42" Box)	67.20	—	31.70	=	35.50	1.30
(48" Box)	104.70	—	40.30	=	64.40	2.40
(54" Box)	132.50	—	56.00	=	76.50	2.83
(60" Box)	190.80	—	74.40	=	116.40	4.30

*Shrinkage Factor not applied. See Table for shrinkage of various soil types.

SOIL EXCAVATION AND BACKFILL

SLOPE MEASUREMENTS

Horizontal Measure		Vertical Measure	Multiplying Factor
3/4	to	1	1.667
1	to	1	1.4142
1 1/2	to	1	1.2019
2	to	1	1.1180
2 1/2	to	1	1.0770
3	to	1	1.0541
4	to	1	1.0308
5	to	1	1.0198

Example—A 2 to 1 slope having a horizontal (Plan) measure of 20 ft.

20 ft. x 1.1180 = 22.360 — the actual measurement of the face of the slope.

ACRES IN AN AREA
Multiply square footage by 23 and mark off 6 decimal places—this gives the number of acres in an area.

APPROXIMATE EQUIVALENCES: SLOPE/GRADE/DEGREE

Slope Ratio*	Percent Grade*	Angle Degrees (Approx.)
Flat	Flat	0
100:1	1%	1
20:1	5%	3
10:1	10%	6
5:1	20%	11
4:1	25%	13
-	30%	16
3:1	33 1/3%	17
-	40%	22
2:1	50%	26
-	60%	31
-	80%	38
1:1	100%	45
Vertical	Vertical	90

*Horizontal to vertical ratio.

TOPSOIL FACTORS FOR PLANT MATERIALS

Tree Size	Dimension of Tree Pit		Ball Size	Ball C.Y.	C.Y. Topsoil in Pit		Factor	
	Topsoil	Stone Block			Topsoil	Stone Block	Topsoil	Stone Block
3' - 4' Ht.	3' Dia. 3' Deep	5' x 5' x 3:	15"	.03	.79	2.78		2.75
4' - 5' Ht.	4' Dia. 3' Deep	5' x 5' x 3'	18"	.05	1.40	2.78		2.73
5' - 6' Ht.	4' Dia. 3' Deep	5' x 5' x 3'	18"	.05	1.40	2.78		2.73
6' - 8' Ht.	4' Dia. 3' Deep	5' x 5' x 3'	18"	.05	1.40	2.78		2.73
8' -10' Ht.	4' Dia. 3' Deep	5' x 5' x 3'	20"	.08	1.40	2.78		2.70
1½"- 2" Cal.	4' Dia. 3' Deep	5' x 5' x 3'	22"	.11	1.40	2.78		2.67
2"- 2½" Cal.	4' Dia. 3' Deep	5' x 5' x 3'	24"	.14	1.40	2.78		2.64
2½"- 3" Cal.	5' Dia. 3' Deep	5' x 5' x 3'	30"	.26	2.18	2.78		2.52
3" - 3½" Cal.	5' Dia. 3' Deep	5' x 5' x 3'	36"	.46	2.18	2.78		2.32
3½"- 4" Cal.	6' Dia. 3' Deep	6' x 6' x 3'	42"	.72	3.14	4.00		3.28
4"- 5" Cal.	6' Dia. 3½ Deep	6' x 6' x 3.5'	48"	1.08	3.67	4.66		3.58
5"- 6" Cal.	7' Dia. 4' Deep	7' x 7' x 4'	60"	2.11	5.70	7.26		5.15
6"- 7" Cal.	8' Dia. 4.5' Deep	8' x 8' x 4.5'	72"	3.64	8.38	10.65		7.01
7"- 8" Cal.	9' Dia. 5' Deep	9' x 9' x 5'	84"	5.79	11.35	15.00		9.31
8"-10" Cal.	10' Dia. 6' Deep	10' x 10' x 6'	96"	8.65	17.50	22.20		11.55
10"-12" Cal.	12' Dia. 6' Deep	12' x 12' x 6'	108"	5.23	25.20	32.00		26.77

NUMBER OF AGRICULTURAL DRAIN PIPES TO THE ACRE
(number of pipes 12 in long: or ft run of pipes)

6 ft apart	7,260	24 ft apart	1,815
9 ft apart	4,840	27 ft apart	1,613
12 ft apart	3,630	30 ft apart	1,452
18 ft apart	2,420	42 ft apart	1,037
21 ft apart	2,074	60 ft apart	726

SOIL: WATER HOLDING CAPACITY
(Expressed as a percentage of weight)

Coarse sandy soil	15—30
Light loam	22—34
Stiff clay	36—50
Sandy peat	53—60

APPROXIMATE SHRINKAGE FACTORS
FOR VARIOUS SOIL TYPES

(calculated from backfill material in a loose, friable state
at time of use and subsequent normal settling)

Soil Type	loose-stockpiled material	normal shrinkage
Sand	1	*1.18
Sandy-Loam	1	1.23
Clay-Loam	1	1.43
Clay	1	1.48

*Explanation: shrinkage factor must be larger than swellage factor to provide for the shrinkage of that material added.

CONSTITUENTS OF SOILS
(main constituents given as a percentage:

	Organic matter	Clay	Sand	Lime	Potash	Phosphoric acid	Alkalies (incl. magnesia)
Fertile loam	4.38	18.09	76.16	1.37	0.49	0.12	—
Orchard soil (under turf)	11.70	48.39	35.95	1.54	0.91	0.08	—
Calcareous clayey soil	11.08	52.06	24.53	11.53	0.32	0.12	—
Heavy clay	4.87	72.29	9.26	1.15	0.06	1.37	—
Sterile sandy soil	5.36	4.57	89.82	0.25	—	(trace)	0.49

EXCAVATION AND TOPSOIL

To find the amount of Excavation and/or Topsoil for Lawn area, multiply the area by the number of inches of depth required and divide by 10. This will give the number of cubic feet required. Divide the answer by 27 to find the number of cubic yards. This manner of figuring will include 20% expansion or shrinkage.

Examples:
1. Area 6432 square feet 3 inches deep
   6432 x 3 = 19,296 divided by 10 = 1929.6 cu. ft. or 71.5 cubic yards

2. Area 288,645 square feet 7 inches deep
   288,645 x 7 = 2,020,515 divided by 10 = 202,051.5 cu. ft. or 7843.4 cubic yards

3. Area 11,988 square feet 3 feet deep
   11,988 x 36 = 431,568 divided by 10 = 43,156.8 cubic feet or 1598.4 cubic yards

Earth expands 20% when loosened up. Topsoil shrinks 20% when compacted. Thus these Figures for lawns can be used for either Excavation or Topsoil as the 20% is included either way.

SOIL EXCAVATION AND BACKFILL

TEXTURAL COMPOSITION OF SOILS

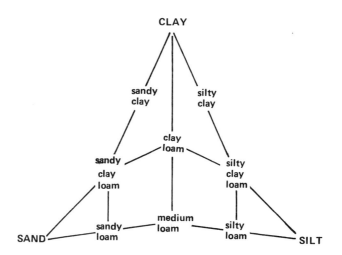

MIXING OF MANURES AND FERTILIZERS

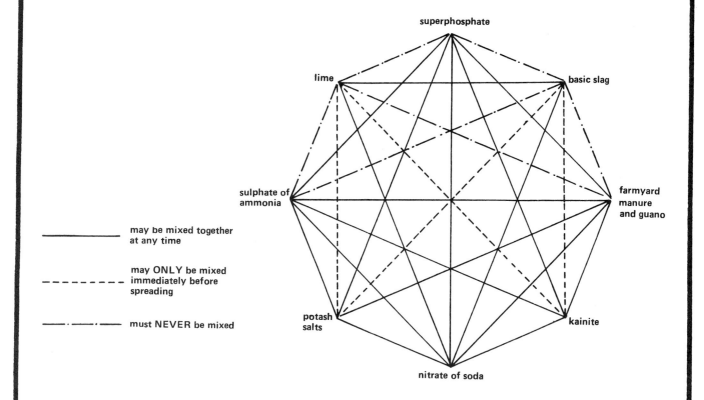

SOIL EXCAVATION AND BACKFILL

VOLUME IN CUBIC YARDS

Example: Area of 50 sq. ft. x 2 in. = ¼ cu. yd.

Depth in inches

SQUARE FEET	2	3	4	6	8	12	CUBIC YARDS
50	¼	½	½	1	1+	2	
100	½	1—	1+	2	2½	4	
150	1	1½	2	3	4	6	
200	1+	2	2½	3½	5	7½	
250	1½	2½	3	4½	6	9	
300	2	3	3½	5½	7½	11	
350	2+	3½	4½	6½	9	13	
400	2½	4	5	7½	10	15	
450	3	4½	5½	8½	11	17	
500	3+	4½	6	9	12	18½	
550	3½	5	7	10	13½	20	
600	3½	5½	7½	11	15	22	
650	4	6	8	12	16	24	
700	4+	6½	8½	13	17	26	
750	4½	7	9½	14	18½	28	
800	5+	7½	10	15	20	30	
850	5	8	10½	15½	21	31	
900	5½	8½	11	17	22	33	
950	6	9	12	17½	23	35	
1,000	6	9	12	18½	25	37	

SOIL EXCAVATION AND BACKFILL

NURSERY CONTAINER STOCK
APPROXIMATE BACK–FILL VOLUME FOR VARIOUS CONTAINER STOCK
SQUARE PLANT–PITS: VERTICAL SIDES

	Plant Pit Volume Cu. Ft.	(minus)	Container Stock Displacement (Cu. Ft.)	(equals)	*Back-Fill Necessary Cu. Ft.	Cu. Yds.
(1 Gal)	.7		.15		.55	0.02
(5 Gal)	3.7		.60		3.10	0.115
(15 Gal)	12.5		2.00		10.50	0.40
(16" Box)	14.2		2.50		11.70	0.43
(20" Box)	22.2		4.75		17.45	0.64
(24" Box)	32.0		6.70		25.30	0.94
(30" Box)	45.5		13.60		31.90	1.20
(36" Box)	80.6		23.40		57.20	2.10
(42" Box)	112.7		31.70		81.00	3.00
(48" Box)	168.7		40.30		128.40	4.75
(54" Box)	216.7		56.00		160.70	5.90
(60" Box)	283.5		74.40		209.10	7.74

*Shrinkage Factor not applied.

SOIL EXCAVATION AND BACKFILL

TREE PITS AND TREE BALLS
Cubic Feet Per Tree
For Estimating Excavation and Top Soil

	Depths (Feet)	1	1 1/4	1 1/2	1 3/4	2	2 1/4	2 1/2	2 3/4	3	3 1/4	3 1/2
						Diameters in Feet						
Tree Pit	1	.94	1.47	2.13	2.88	3.77	4.78	5.89	7.13	8.48	9.96	11.5
Tree Ball		.68	1.07	1.54	2.10	2.73	3.42	4.30	5.20	6.19	7.38	8.4
Tree Pit	1 1/4	1.16	1.85	2.65	3.60	4.71	5.93	7.37	8.90	10.6	12.4	14.4
Tree Ball		.85	1.35	1.93	2.63	3.42	4.29	5.36	6.49	7.7	9.2	10.5
Tree Pit	1 1/2	1.40	2.22	3.18	4.32	5.65	7.16	8.83	10.7	12.7	15.0	17.3
Tree Ball		1.02	1.62	2.32	3.15	4.10	5.19	6.39	7.8	9.2	10.9	12.7
Tree Pit	1 3/4	1.65	2.58	3.70	5.04	6.60	8.20	10.3	12.5	14.8	17.4	20.2
Tree Ball		1.29	1.88	2.72	3.68	4.78	6.03	7.5	9.1	10.7	12.7	14.7
Tree Pit	2	1.87	2.95	4.26	5.76	7.54	9.55	11.8	14.3	17.0	19.9	23.0
Tree Ball		1.38	2.15	3.10	4.20	5.49	6.92	8.5	10.4	12.3	14.5	16.8
Tree Pit	2 1/4	2.10	3.32	4.78	6.48	8.48	10.7	13.2	16.0	19.1	22.4	26.0
Tree Ball		1.55	2.43	3.48	4.73	6.19	7.8	9.6	11.7	13.8	16.4	18.9
Tree Pit	2 1/2	2.34	3.69	5.30	7.20	9.42	11.9	14.7	17.8	21.2	24.9	28.9
Tree Ball		1.70	2.70	3.87	5.25	6.89	8.7	10.7	13.0	15.4	18.2	21.0
Tree Pit	2 3/4	2.57	4.06	5.83	7.92	10.3	13.1	16.2	19.6	23.3	27.4	31.8
Tree Ball		1.87	2.98	4.25	5.77	7.6	9.6	11.8	14.3	17.0	20.0	23.1
Tree Pit	3	2.81	4.43	6.37	8.64	11.3	14.3	17.7	21.4	25.4	29.9	34.6
Tree Ball		2.05	3.24	4.65	6.30	8.3	10.5	12.9	15.6	18.6	21.8	25.2
Tree Pit	3 1/4	3.00	4.80	6.90	9.36	12.2	15.5	19.2	23.3	27.5	32.4	37.5
Tree Ball		2.21	3.50	5.03	6.83	8.9	11.4	14.0	16.9	20.1	23.6	27.3
Tree Pit	3 1/2	3.28	5.17	7.41	10.1	13.2	16.7	20.7	25.0	29.6	34.9	40.4
Tree Ball		2.39	3.77	5.42	7.4	9.6	12.2	15.0	18.2	21.7	25.4	29.4
Tree Pit	3 3/4	3.50	5.53	7.96	10.8	14.2	17.9	22.2	26.7	31.7	37.1	43.3
Tree Ball		2.56	4.04	5.80	7.9	10.3	13.1	16.1	19.5	23.2	27.2	31.5
Tree Pit	4	3.74	5.90	8.50	11.5	15.1	19.1	23.7	28.5	33.8	39.9	46.2
Tree Ball		2.72	4.31	6.19	8.4	11.0	14.0	17.2	20.8	24.8	29.0	33.6
Tree Pit	4 1/4	3.97	6.28	9.01	12.3	16.0	20.3	25.1	30.3	36.0	42.3	49.1
Tree Ball		2.90	4.58	6.58	8.9	11.8	14.8	18.3	22.1	26.3	30.8	35.7
Tree Pit	4 1/2	4.20	6.64	9.55	13.0	17.0	21.5	26.6	32.0	38.1	44.8	52.0
Tree Ball		3.07	4.85	6.97	9.5	12.4	15.7	19.4	23.4	27.8	32.6	37.8
Tree Pit	4 3/4	4.43	7.00	10.0	13.7	17.9	22.7	28.0	33.8	40.2	47.3	54.9
Tree Ball		3.24	5.12	7.4	10.0	13.0	16.5	20.4	24.7	29.1	34.2	40.0
Tree Pit	5	4.68	7.38	10.6	14.4	18.8	23.9	29.8	35.6	42.3	49.9	57.7
Tree Ball		3.41	5.38	7.8	10.5	13.7	17.4	21.5	26.0	30.9	26.1	42.1
Tree Pit	5 1/2	5.14	8.12	11.7	15.8	20.7	26.3	32.4	39.2	46.7	54.8	63.5
Tree Ball		3.76	5.93	8.5	11.6	15.1	19.1	23.7	28.6	34.0	40.0	46.3
Tree Pit	6	5.61	8.86	12.7	17.3	22.6	28.7	35.4	42.8	50.9	57.8	69.3
Tree Ball		4.10	6.46	9.3	12.6	16.5	20.9	25.9	31.2	27.1	43.6	50.5

TREE PITS AND TREE BALLS
Cubic Feet Per Tree
For Estimating Excavation and Top Soil

	Depths (Feet)	3 3/4	4	4 1/4	4 1/2	4 3/4	5	5 1/2	6	6 1/2	7	7 1/2
						Diameters in Feet						
Tree Pit	1	13.3	15.1	17.0	19.1	21.2	23.6	28.5	33.9	39.8	46.2	53.0
Tree Ball		9.7	11.0	12.4	13.9	15.5	17.4	20.8	24.7	29.0	33.7	38.7
Tree Pit	1 1/4	16.6	18.8	21.3	23.8	26.5	29.5	35.6	42.4	49.8	57.7	66.3
Tree Ball		12.2	13.8	15.5	17.4	19.4	21.7	26.0	30.9	36.3	42.1	48.3
Tree Pit	1 1/2	19.9	22.6	25.5	28.6	31.9	35.4	42.8	50.9	59.7	69.3	79.5
Tree Ball		14.5	16.5	18.6	20.9	23.2	25.8	31.2	37.1	43.6	50.5	58.0
Tree Pit	1 3/4	23.2	26.4	29.7	33.4	37.2	41.2	49.9	59.4	69.7	80.8	92.8
Tree Ball		16.9	19.1	21.7	24.4	27.1	30.1	36.4	43.4	50.8	58.9	67.7
Tree Pit	2	26.5	30.2	34.0	38.2	42.0	47.1	57.0	67.9	79.6	92.4	106.1
Tree Ball		19.2	21.9	24.8	27.8	31.0	34.4	41.6	49.5	58.1	67.4	77.3
Tree Pit	2 1/4	29.8	33.9	38.3	43.0	47.8	53.0	64.1	76.4	89.6	103.9	119.3
Tree Ball		21.6	24.6	27.9	31.3	34.9	39.7	46.8	55.7	65.3	75.8	87.0
Tree Pit	2 1/2	33.1	37.7	42.5	47.7	53.1	59.0	71.3	84.9	99.6	115.5	132.6
Tree Ball		24.1	27.3	31.0	34.7	38.8	43.0	52.0	61.9	72.6	84.2	96.7
Tree Pit	2 3/4	36.5	41.5	46.8	52.5	58.5	64.8	78.4	93.3	109.5	127.0	145.8
Tree Ball		26.4	30.0	34.1	38.1	42.6	47.3	57.2	68.0	79.9	92.6	106.3
Tree Pit	3	39.8	45.3	51.0	57.3	63.8	70.6	85.5	101.8	119.5	138.5	159.0
Tree Ball		28.8	32.8	37.0	41.5	46.5	51.6	62.3	74.2	87.1	101.0	116.0
Tree Pit	3 1/4	43.1	49.0	55.3	62.0	69.1	76.5	92.6	110.3	129.4	150.1	172.3
Tree Ball		31.4	35.7	40.1	45.0	50.4	55.9	67.5	80.4	94.4	109.5	125.6
Tree Pit	3 1/2	46.4	52.8	59.6	66.8	74.3	82.5	99.7	118.7	139.4	161.7	185.6
Tree Ball		33.9	38.5	43.2	48.5	54.4	60.2	72.7	86.6	101.6	117.9	135.3
Tree Pit	3 3/4	49.7	56.6	63.8	71.6	79.7	88.4	106.8	127.3	149.3	173.2	198.8
Tree Ball		36.4	41.2	46.3	52.2	58.1	64.4	77.5	92.3	108.7	126.3	145.0
Tree Pit	4	53.0	60.3	68.1	76.3	85.0	94.2	113.9	135.7	159.3	184.8	212.1
Tree Ball		38.9	44.0	49.4	55.7	62.0	68.7	82.8	98.5	116.1	134.7	154.6
Tree Pit	4 1/4	56.3	64.1	72.3	81.1	90.3	100.1	121.0	144.2	169.2	196.3	225.3
Tree Ball		41.4	46.8	52.5	59.2	65.9	73.0	88.1	104.8	123.0	142.4	163.4
Tree Pit	4 1/2	59.6	67.9	76.6	85.9	95.6	106.2	128.2	152.7	179.2	207.9	238.6
Tree Ball		43.9	49.5	55.6	62.7	69.8	77.4	93.4	111.0	130.3	150.9	172.9
Tree Pit	4 3/4	63.0	71.6	80.9	90.7	101.0	112.0	135.3	161.2	189.1	219.4	251.9
Tree Ball		46.0	52.3	58.8	66.2	73.7	81.7	98.6	117.2	137.6	159.7	182.4
Tree Pit	5	66.3	75.4	85.2	95.5	106.3	117.9	142.5	169.7	199.1	230.9	265.1
Tree Ball		48.5	55.0	62.0	69.7	77.5	86.0	103.9	123.4	144.9	168.2	192.0
Tree Pit	5 1/2	72.9	83.0	93.6	105.2	116.9	129.6	156.8	186.7	219.0	254.0	291.6
Tree Ball		53.2	60.5	68.3	76.6	85.2	94.6	114.2	135.9	159.6	184.6	211.0
Tree Pit	6	79.5	90.5	102.1	114.5	127.5	141.5	171.0	203.6	238.9	277.1	318.1
Tree Ball		58.0	66.0	74.5	83.5	93.0	103.1	124.7	148.5	174.2	202.0	230.0

SOIL EXCAVATION AND BACKFILL

TREE PITS AND TREE BALLS
Cubic Feet Per Tree
For Estimating Excavation and Top Soil

	Depths (Feet)	\multicolumn{12}{c}{Diameters in Feet}										
		8	8 1/2	9	9 1/2	10	10 1/2	11	11 1/2	12	12 1/2	13
Tree Pit	1	60.3	68.1	76.3	85.1	94.3	103.7	114.0	124.8	135.7	147.3	159.3
Tree Ball		44.0	49.7	55.7	62.0	68.7	75.8	85.2	91.1	99.4	107.4	116.1
Tree Pit	1 1/4	75.4	85.1	95.4	106.3	117.8	129.6	142.6	156.0	169.6	184.1	199.1
Tree Ball		55.0	62.1	69.6	77.5	85.9	94.5	103.9	113.8	124.2	134.2	145.2
Tree Pit	1 1/2	90.5	102.2	114.5	127.6	141.4	155.5	171.1	187.2	203.6	220.9	238.9
Tree Ball		66.0	74.5	83.5	93.0	103.8	113.4	124.7	136.6	148.9	161.1	174.2
Tree Pit	1 3/4	105.6	119.2	133.6	148.9	165.0	181.4	199.6	218.4	237.5	257.7	278.7
Tree Ball		77.0	86.9	97.4	108.5	120.3	132.3	145.6	159.3	173.6	187.9	203.2
Tree Pit	2	120.6	136.2	152.7	170.1	188.5	207.4	288.1	249.3	271.4	294.3	318.6
Tree Ball		88.0	99.3	111.3	124.0	137.5	151.2	166.3	182.1	198.3	214.8	232.3
Tree Pit	2 1/4	135.7	153.2	171.8	191.4	212.1	233.3	256.6	280.5	305.4	331.3	358.4
Tree Ball		99.0	111.7	125.2	139.5	154.6	170.1	187.1	204.9	223.0	241.6	261.3
Tree Pit	2 1/2	150.8	170.2	190.9	212.6	235.6	259.2	285.1	311.6	339.3	368.2	398.2
Tree Ball		110.0	124.1	139.2	155.1	171.8	189.0	207.9	227.6	247.7	268.3	290.3
Tree Pit	2 3/4	165.9	187.3	210.0	233.9	259.2	285.1	313.6	342.7	373.2	405.0	438.0
Tree Ball		121.0	136.6	153.0	170.8	189.0	207.9	228.7	250.4	272.5	295.2	319.4
Tree Pit	3	181.0	204.3	229.0	255.2	282.7	311.0	342.1	373.9	407.1	441.8	477.8
Tree Ball		132.0	149.0	167.0	186.1	206.2	226.8	249.5	273.1	297.2	322.1	348.4
Tree Pit	3 1/4	196.1	221.3	248.1	276.4	306.3	337.0	370.6	405.0	441.0	478.6	517.6
Tree Ball		143.0	161.4	180.9	201.6	223.3	245.7	270.3	295.9	322.0	348.8	377.4
Tree Pit	3 1/2	211.1	238.4	267.2	297.7	329.9	362.9	399.1	436.1	475.0	515.4	557.5
Tree Ball		154.0	173.8	194.8	217.1	240.5	264.6	291.1	318.7	346.6	375.7	406.5
Tree Pit	3 3/4	226.2	255.4	286.3	319.0	353.4	388.8	427.6	467.2	508.9	552.2	597.3
Tree Ball		165.0	186.2	308.8	232.6	257.7	283.5	311.8	341.4	371.2	402.5	435.5
Tree Pit	4	241.3	272.4	305.4	340.2	377.0	414.7	456.1	498.5	542.8	589.0	637.1
Tree Ball		176.0	198.6	222.7	248.1	274.9	302.4	332.6	364.2	395.8	429.3	464.5
Tree Pit	4 1/4	256.4	289.4	324.5	361.5	400.6	440.6	484.6	529.7	576.8	625.8	676.9
Tree Ball		187.0	211.0	236.7	263.6	292.1	321.3	353.4	386.9	420.4	456.2	493.6
Tree Pit	4 1/2	271.5	306.5	343.5	382.7	424.1	466.6	513.1	561.0	610.7	662.7	716.7
Tree Ball		198.0	223.4	250.5	279.1	309.3	340.2	374.2	409.8	445.5	483.0	522.6
Tree Pit	4 3/4	286.6	323.5	362.6	404.0	447.7	492.5	541.6	592.0	644.6	699.5	756.6
Tree Ball		209.0	235.8	264.4	294.6	326.5	359.1	395.0	432.6	470.0	509.8	551.6
Tree Pit	5	301.7	340.5	381.7	425.3	471.2	518.4	570.2	623.2	678.5	736.3	796.4
Tree Ball		220.0	248.3	278.3	310.0	343.7	378.0	415.8	455.3	489.8	536.7	580.8
Tree Pit	5 1/2	331.8	374.6	419.9	467.8	518.4	570.2	627.2	685.5	746.4	810.0	876.0
Tree Ball		243.0	273.1	306.2	341.1	378.1	415.8	457.4	500.8	544.0	590.4	638.7
Tree Pit	6	362.6	408.6	458.0	510.3	565.5	622.1	684.2	747.9	814.2	883.6	955.7
Tree Ball		264.0	297.9	334.0	372.2	412.5	453.6	499.0	546.3	593.8	644.0	696.8

SOIL EXCAVATION AND BACKFILL

TREE PITS AND TREE BALLS
Cubic Feet Per Tree
For Estimating Excavation and Top Soil

	Depths (Feet)	Diameters in Feet								
		13 1/2	14	15	16	17	18	19	20	21
Tree Pit	1	171.7	184.7	212.0	241.3	272.4	305.4	340.2	377.0	415.6
Tree Ball		125.3	134.7	154.6	175.9	198.6	222.7	248.1	274.9	303.1
Tree Pit	1 1/4	214.7	230.9	265.1	301.6	340.5	381.7	425.3	471.2	519.4
Tree Ball		156.6	168.4	193.3	219.9	248.3	278.3	310.1	343.6	378.9
Tree Pit	1 1/2	257.7	277.0	318.1	361.9	408.5	458.0	510.3	565.5	623.5
Tree Ball		187.9	202.0	231.9	263.9	297.9	334.0	372.1	412.3	454.6
Tree Pit	1 3/4	300.6	323.2	371.0	422.2	476.6	534.4	595.4	659.7	727.4
Tree Ball		219.2	234.7	270.6	307.9	347.6	389.7	434.2	481.1	530.4
Tree Pit	2	343.5	369.2	424.0	482.5	544.7	610.7	680.4	754.0	831.3
Tree Ball		250.5	269.4	309.3	351.9	397.2	445.3	497.2	549.8	606.1
Tree Pit	2 1/4	386.5	415.4	477.0	542.8	612.8	681.7	765.5	848.2	935.2
Tree Ball		281.8	303.1	347.9	395.8	446.9	501.0	558.2	618.5	681.8
Tree Pit	2 1/2	429.4	461.6	530.0	603.1	680.8	763.4	850.5	942.5	1039.1
Tree Ball		313.1	336.8	386.6	439.8	496.5	556.7	620.2	687.2	757.6
Tree Pit	2 3/4	472.4	507.9	583.1	663.4	748.9	839.8	935.6	1036.7	1142.9
Tree Ball		344.4	370.4	425.2	483.8	546.2	612.4	682.2	755.9	833.4
Tree Pit	3	515.3	554.0	636.1	723.8	817.0	916.1	1020.6	1131.0	1426.8
Tree Ball		375.7	404.1	463.9	527.8	595.8	668.0	744.3	824.7	909.2
Tree Pit	3 1/4	558.3	600.2	689.1	784.1	885.1	992.4	1105.7	1225.2	1350.7
Tree Ball		407.1	437.8	502.6	571.8	645.5	723.7	806.3	893.4	984.9
Tree Pit	3 1/2	601.2	646.4	742.1	844.5	953.1	1068.7	1190.7	1319.5	1454.6
Tree Ball		438.4	471.5	541.2	615.7	695.1	779.4	868.3	962.1	1060.7
Tree Pit	3 3/4	644.2	692.5	795.1	904.8	1021.2	1145.0	1275.8	1413.7	1558.5
Tree Ball		469.7	505.2	579.9	659.7	744.8	835.0	930.3	1030.8	1136.5
Tree Pit	4	687.1	738.7	848.2	965.1	1089.3	1221.4	1360.8	1508.0	1662.5
Tree Ball		501.0	538.8	618.5	709.7	794.4	890.7	992.3	1099.5	1212.2
Tree Pit	4 1/4	730.0	785.0	901.2	1025.4	1157.4	1297.7	1445.9	1602.2	1766.4
Tree Ball		532.3	572.5	657.2	747.7	844.1	946.4	1054.4	1168.3	1288.0
Tree Pit	4 1/2	772.9	831.2	954.2	1085.7	1225.4	1374.1	1531.0	1696.5	1870.3
Tree Ball		563.6	606.2	695.9	791.7	890.7	1002.0	1116.4	1232.0	1363.8
Tree Pit	4 3/4	815.8	877.5	1007.2	1146.0	1293.5	1450.4	1616.0	1790.7	1974.2
Tree Ball		595.0	639.9	734.5	835.6	943.4	1057.7	1178.4	1305.7	1439.5
Tree Pit	5	858.8	923.6	1060.2	1206.3	1361.7	1526.8	1701.0	1885.0	2078.1
Tree Ball		626.3	673.6	773.2	879.6	993.0	1113.4	1240.4	1374.4	1515.2
Tree Pit	5 1/2	944.7	1016.0	1166.3	1326.9	1498.0	1679.5	1871.2	2073.5	2285.9
Tree Ball		688.9	740.9	850.5	967.6	1092.3	1224.7	1364.5	1511.9	1666.9
Tree Pit	6	1030.6	1108.4	1272.3	1447.6	1634.2	1832.2	2041.4	2262.0	2493.7
Tree Ball		751.5	808.2	927.8	1055.5	1191.6	1336.0	1488.5	1649.3	1818.4

SOIL EXCAVATION AND BACKFILL

FERTILIZERS
AND
SOIL
ADDITIVES

CHART OF CONVERSIONS

For Dry Insecticides				
For 100 gallons of water	For 50 gallons of water	For 25 gallons of water	For 6 1/4 gallons of water	For 3 1/8 gallons of water
1 pound	8 ounces	4 ounces	1 ounce	1 T.
2 pounds	1 pound	8 ounces	2 ounces	2 T.
4 pounds	2 pounds	1 pound	4 ounces	4 T.

For Liquid Insecticides

For 100 gallons of water	For 50 gallons of water	For 25 gallons of water	For 6 1/4 gallons of water	For 3 1/8 gallons of water
1/2 pint	1/2 pint (4 fl. oz.)	4 T. (2 fl. oz.)	1 T. (1/2 fl. oz.)	1/2 T. (1/4 fl. oz.)
1 pint	1/2 pint (8 fl. oz.)	1/4 pint (4 fl. oz.)	2 T. (1 fl. oz.)	1 T. (1/2 fl. oz.)
1 quart	1 pint (16 fl. oz.)	1/2 pint (8 fl. oz.)	4 T. (2 fl. oz.)	2 T. (1 fl. oz.)

T. = 1 level tablespoon

TABLE OF EQUIVALENTS

Equivalent Quantitites for Liquid Insecticides and Fungicides in Water

Water	1 to 25 (4%)	1 to 50 (2%)	1 to 100 (%)	1 to 200 (1/2 %)	1 to 400 (1/4%)	1 to 800 (1/8%)
1 Gallon	5.12 oz.	2.56 oz.	1.28 oz.	.64 oz.	.32 oz.	.16 oz.
3 Gallons	15.56 oz.	7.8 oz.	(3 tbs.)	(4 tsp)	(2 tsp.)	(1 tsp.)
	(1/3 pt.)	(5 1/4 tbs.)	3.84 oz.	1.92 oz.	.96 oz.	.48 oz.
	(1 pt.)	(1/2 pt.)	(1/4 pt.)	(4 tbs.)	(6 tsp.)	(3 tsp.)
5 Gallons	25.6 oz.	12.8 oz.	6.4 oz.	3.2 oz.	1.6 oz.	.8 oz.
	(1 2/3 pts.)	(1 1/2 cups)	(3/4 cup)	(6 1/2 tbs.)	(3 1/2 tbs.)	(5 tsp.)
100 Gallons	(4 gals.)	(2 gals.)	(1 gal.)	(2 qts.)	(1 qt.)	(1 pt.)

FERTILIZERS AND SOIL ADDITIVES

CONVERSION TABLES – PESTICIDE APPLICATION RATES

100 GALLON RATE EQUIVALENTS

FOR DRY INSECTICIDES

100 Gal. Water	50 Gal. Water	25 Gal. Water	6 1/4 Gal. Water	3 1/8 Gal. Water
1 lb.	8 oz.	4 oz.	1 oz.	1 T.
2 lb.	1 lb.	8 oz.	2 oz.	2 T.
4 lb.	2 lb.	1 lb.	4 oz.	4 T.

FOR LIQUID INSECTICIDES

1/2 pt.	1/4 pt. (4 fl. oz.)	4 T. (2 fl. oz.)	1 T. (1/2 fl. oz.)	1/2 T. (1/4 fl. oz.)
1 pt.	1/2 pt. (8 fl. oz.)	1/4 pt. (4 fl. oz.)	2 T. (1 fl. oz.)	1 T. (1/2 fl. oz.)
1 qt.	1 pt. (16 fl. oz.)	1/2 pt. (8 fl. oz.)	4 T. (2 fl. oz.)	2 T. (1 fl. oz.)

T = One level tablespoon

3 teaspoons = 1 tablespoon
2 tablespoons = 1 fluid oz.
1 cup = 8 fluid oz.
1 pt. = 2 cups = 16 fl. oz.
2 pts. = 1 quart

4 quarts = 1 gallon
1 lb. = 32 tablespoons
1 qt. = 64 tablespoons
1 gal. = 8-10 lbs.
1 quart = 2 - 2 1/2 lbs.

FERTILIZERS AND SOIL ADDITIVES

CONVERSION TABLE FOR SMALL QUANTITIES OF SPRAY MATERIALS

(T = Tablespoon, t = teaspoon)

Amount per 100 gal.	Amount per 1 gal.	Amount per 100 gal.	Amount per 1 gal.
(Liquids)	(Liquids)	(Liquids)	(Liquids)
1/4 pt.	1/4 t.	1/2 lb.	1/2 t.
1 pt.	1 t.	1 lb.	1 t.
1 1/2 pt.	1 1/2 t.	2 lb.	2 t.
1 qt.	2 t.	3 lb.	1 T.
3 pt.	3 t.	4 lb.	1 1/3 T.
1 gal.	2 1/2 T.	6 lb.	2 T.
2 gal.	5 T.	10 lb.	3 T.
3 gal.	1/2 cup	16 lb.	5 1/2 T.
4 gal.	2/3 cup	18 lb.	6 T.
5 gal.	1 cup	20 lb.	6 2/3 T.

TABLE OF EQUIVALENTS FOR LIQUID MEASURE (VOLUME)

Gal.	Qts.	Pts.	Fluid Oz.	Cupsful	Table spoonful	Tea spoonful	Milliliters
1	4	8	128	16			
	1	2	32	4			
		1	16	2	32		
			1	1/8	2	6	30
				1	16	48	240
					1	3	15
						1	5

SOIL MIXES
Organic Materials For Six-Inch Depth Per 1,000 Square Feet*

Desired Percentage of Organic Material Volume in Mix	Approximate Thickness Applied to Soil Surfaces in Inches	Cubic Yards of Organic Materials Necessary per 1,000 Square Feet
5	.33	1.0
10	.67	2.0
15	1.00	3.0
20	1.33	4.0
25	1.67	5.0
30	2.00	6.0
35	2.33	7.0
40	2.67	8.0
45	3.00	9.0
50	3.33	10.0

*Figures are approximate due to variance in volume of organic materials used.

Example: 20% organic material is to be incorporated into the top six inches of a 2,500 square foot area.
From the chart, find that the organic material must be applied to a depth of 1 1/3″ and 10 Cubic Yards (4 x 2.5) will be needed.

APPROXIMATE WEIGHTS OF COMMON FERTILIZERS, DRY
(For use only when scale is missing)

Materials measuring 1 1/2 cupfuls per pound (24 tablespoons):

Ground limestone   Nitrate of soda, granular (15-0-0)
Sulfate of potash (0-0-50)

Materials measuring 2 cupfuls per pound (32 tablespoons)

Calcium nitrate (15-0-0)

Materials measuring 2 1/4 cupfuls per pound (36 tablespoons)

Superphosphate (0-20-0)   Muriate of potash (0-0-50)
Treble superphosphate 0-45-0)   Nitrate of potash (13-0-44)
Complete (4-12-8)   Complete (5-10-5)

Material measuring 2 1/2 cupfuls per pound (40 tablespoons)

Ammonium nitrate (granular) (33-0-0)
Epsom salts (magnesium)

Materials measuring 2 3/4 cupfuls per pound (44 tablespoons)

Ammonium sulfate (20-0-0)
Ammonium phosphate (mono) (11-48-0)
Aluminum sulfate (Acidifying)
Borax (granular) (Boron)

Materials measuring 4 cupfuls per pound (64 tablespoons)

Lime, hydrated (Calcium)
Sulfur (Acidifying)

WEIGHTS AND COVERAGES OF MATERIALS

Topsoil
6 wheelbarrow loads equal one cubic yard.
1 cubic yard loose weighs 2,000 pounds.
1 cubic yard compacted weighs 2,400 pounds.
1 cubic yard loose will cover:

324 square feet 1" deep	36 square feet 9" deep
162 square feet 2" deep	32 square feet 10" deep
108 square feet 3" deep	27 square feet 12" deep
81 square feet 4" deep	21 square feet 15" deep
54 square feet 6" deep	18 square feet 18" deep
40 square feet 8" deep	13 square feet 24" deep

One acre requiring topsoil 6" deep will take 807 cubic yards loose.
Add 20% for compacting.

Peat Moss
1 bale contains 20 to 22 bushels compacted. When broken up
and loosened, one bale will cover:

240 square feet 1" deep
120 square feet 2" deep
80 square feet 3" deep

One acre of ground requiring a mulch of 2" Peat Moss will take 363 bales.

Manure
(Rotted) 1 cubic yard average weight 800 pounds.

Humus
1 cubic yard average weight 1,050 pounds.
To figure quantities use same as Topsoil.

WEIGHTS AND COVERAGES OF MATERIALS

Soil
1 cu. yd. will cover 324 sq. ft. 1" deep.
1 cu. yd. will cover 102 sq. ft. 2" deep.
1 cu. yd. will cover 108 sq. ft. 3" deep.
1 cu. yd. will cover 81 sq. ft. 4" deep.
1 cu. yd. will cover 54 sq. ft. 6" deep.
1 cu. yd. will cover 40 sq. ft. 8" deep.
1 cu. yd. will cover 27 sq. ft. 12" deep.

Granite
1 cu. yd. will cover 300 sq. ft. 1" deep.
1 cu. yd. will cover 150 sq. ft. 2" deep.
1 cu. yd. will cover 100 sq. ft. 3" deep.

Steer Manure
1 sack will cover 175 sq. ft. 1/8" deep.
1 sack will cover 27 sq. ft. 1" deep.
1 sack will cover 13.5 sq. ft. 2" deep.
1 sack will cover 9 sq. ft. 3" deep.

Peat Moss
7½ cu. ft. bale covers 585 sq. ft. 1/6" deep.
7½ cu. ft. bale covers 90 sq. ft. 1" deep.
7½ cu. ft. bale covers 45 sq. ft. 2" deep.
7½ cu. ft. bale covers 30 sq. ft. 3" deep.
11 cu. ft. bale covers 875 sq. ft. 1/6" deep.
11 cu. ft. bale covers 135 sq. ft. 1" deep.
11 cu. ft. bale covers 67.5 sq. ft. 2" deep.
11 cu. ft. bale covers 45 sq. ft. 3" deep.

Bean Straw
1 bale will cover 200 sq. ft. 1" deep.

Milorganite, etc.
1 sack will cover 2,000 sq. ft.

Humisite
1 sack will cover 600 sq. ft.

Nitrohumus
1 sack will cover 300 sq. ft.

WORKABLE CONVERSIONS FOR SOIL AREAS

1 ounce per square foot equals 2,722.5 pounds per acre.
1 ounce per square yard equals 302.5 pounds per acre.
1 ounce per 100 square feet equals 27.2 pounds per acre.
1 pound per 100 square feet equals 435.6 pounds per acre.
1 pound per 1,000 square feet equals 43.6 pounds per acre.
1 pound per acre equals 1/3 ounce per 1,000 square feet.
5 gallons per acre equals 1 pint per 1,000 square feet.
100 gallons per acre equals 2.5 gallons per 1,000 square feet.
100 gallons per acre equals 1 quart per 100 square feet.
100 gallons per acre equals 2.5 pounds per 1,000 square feet.

FERTILIZER SPECIFICATIONS

Shall be of granular or of pellet type, for proper application with cyclone type spreader.

Shall be available in convenient package units (25 lbs. to 50 lbs.).

Shall be a product registered with the state and have a total declaration of contents, both rates and ratios of the ingredients listed on the label.

The nitrogen content shall not be below 6%. The phosphate content shall not exceed the nitrogen content and the potash shall not go below one-half of the nitrogen content.

The preferred ratio shall be a 3:1:2 for nitrogen to phosphate to potash or a close proximation to this (such as 15:5:10, 24:8:16, or 6:2:4, etc.). This is basically how lawn and landscape shrubs remove nutrients from the soil.

Exaggerated claims of coverage or super powers shall be discounted. Soil conditioners, as such, should be avoided unless proven of need.

Price should not exceed 75 cents per pound of actual nitrogen in the bag or container. That is, a 6:10:4 fertilizer will contain three pounds of actual nitrogen (N) in a 50 pound bag. That bag should not exceed $2.25. A 50 pound bag of 22:7:14 will contain 11 pounds of actual N. This bag should not exceed $8.25 to be competitive. Your material should include adequate phosphate and potash in the mixture. Keep it in the 3:1:2 ratio.

Except for unusual conditions, there is very little value, for general use, in using liquid fertilizers or 100% immediately soluble materials.

Plan no less than 4 pounds of actual nitrogen per 1,000 square feet of lawn per year, split into no less than two applications.

PRINCIPAL CONSTITUENTS OF MANURES
(Figures given are average gross percentages.)

	Water	Organic Matter	Nitrogen (or Ammonia)	Phosphoric Acid or Phosphates	Potash	Lime	Magnesium
Farmyard manure	72.6	27.4	0.77	0.39	0.6		
Poultry manure (dried)	7		4	2.3	1.2		
Hoof and horn			12.5	1.0			
Dried blood			12.5				
Bone meal			3.7	22			
"Improved" blood, meat and bone meal			3	9	5		
Fish meal	14	50	4.5	9	5	12	
Wood ash				2.8	9	4.3	3.8
Sewage sludge (dried)	5 - 10		2.0	2.0			
Sewage sludge (activated)	5 - 10		6.0	3.0	0.5		
Spent mushroom beds			1.0	0.7	1.5		
Basic slag				15		45	
Guano (very variable)	5 - 20	7 - 40	2 - 14	40 av.	0.5 - 3.0	10 - 40	
Human feces	77	20	1	1.1	0.3	0.6	0.5
Garden compost (av.)	10 - 15	10 - 20	0.8	0.45	1.45	1.25	0.3

FERTILIZERS AND SOIL ADDITIVES

CHART NO. 2
USE THIS AMOUNT OF ACTUAL MATERIAL IN POUNDS—PER 1000 SQ. FT.
WHEN PERCENT OF CONTENT IS . . .

Where total nutrient need is indicated (check left column), read across top row
to formulation % column as listed. Chart will then give you the total quantity of material needed
to give the actual quantity desired (in lbs./1000 sq. ft.).

To Get This Pound Rate/ 1000 Sq. Ft.	1%	4%	6%	10%	16%	21%	24%	34%	44%	51%	60%	To Get This Rate/Acre (Approx.)
0.25	25	6.25	4.17	2.5	1.56	1.20	1.04	.74	.57	.49	.42	10.89
0.5	50	12.5	8.33	5.0	3.13	2.38	2.08	1.47	1.14	.98	.83	21.78
1.0	100	25.0	16.7	10.0	6.25	4.76	4.16	2.94	2.27	1.96	1.67	43.56
1.5	150	37.5	25.0	15.0	9.37	7.14	6.25	4.41	3.41	2.94	2.50	65.34
2.0	200	50.0	33.3	20.0	12.5	9.5	8.33	5.88	4.54	3.93	3.33	87.12
3.0	300	75.0	50.0	30.0	18.75	14.28	12.5	8.82	6.81	5.88	5.0	130.68
4.0	400	100.0	66.7	40.0	25.0	19.04	16.67	11.76	9.09	7.84	6.67	174.24
5.0	500	125.0	83.3	50.0	31.25	23.8	20.8	14.7	11.36	9.80	8.33	217.80
10.0	1000	250.0	166.7	100.0	62.5	47.6	41.6	29.4	22.07	19.6	16.67	435.6

PEAT MOSS
Coverage: Depth in Inches per Square Surface Footage

*Bale (Compressed) 5.6 Cu. Ft. When Loosened Will Cover:		*Bale (Compressed) 4.0 Cu. Ft. When Loosened Will Cover:	
Depth Inches	Coverage Square Feet	Depth Inches	Coverage Square Feet
.25"	480.0 sq. ft.	.25"	345.6 sq. ft.
.50"	240.0 sq. ft.	.50"	172.8 sq. ft.
1.00"	120.0 sq. ft.	1.00"	86.4 sq. ft.
2.00"	60.0 sq. ft.	2.00"	43.2 sq. ft.
3.00"	40.0 sq. ft.	3.00"	28.8 sq. ft.
4.00"	30.0 sq. ft.	4.00"	21.6 sq. ft.
6.00"	20.0 sq. ft.	6.00"	14.4 sq. ft.
12.00"	10.0 sq. ft.	12.00"	7.2 sq. ft.

*Approximate expansion is 1.8 of compressed volume.

Actual cash value of these nutrients will require checking into local selling prices for your area.

For rough formulation evaluation, get the price per lb. of actual N, P_2O_5 or K_2O. This is done by dividing the cost of the basic material per bag by the % (percent) of material in the bag:

Amonium Sulfato	21%	N
Amonium Nitrate	34%	N
Blood Meal	13%	N
Muriate of Potash	60%	K_2O
Potasium Sulfate	51%	K_2O
Treble Super Phos.	44%	P_2O_5

Amonium Sulfate — 80 lbs. — $3.95 or $3.95 ÷ 21% of 80 lbs.

Or $\dfrac{\$3.95}{16.8 \text{ lbs.}}$ = 23.6 cents/lb. of actual nitrogen.

In general it will be found that N costs approximately 3 times as much as K_2O and that P_2O_5 costs about 2 times as much as K_2O.

This would give N an approximate value of about 24 cents, P_2O_5 a value of 16 cents and K_2O a value of about 8 cents.

To be more exact, price out all basic ingredients to cents per pound and insert into this formula:

$$XA + YB + ZC = \text{value of 100 lbs. of mix}$$

X = cost/ lb. of actual N	A = % of N in formulation
Y = cost/lb. of P_2O_5	B = % of P_2O_5 in formulation
Z = cost/lb. of K_2O	C = % of K_2O in formulation

ACTUAL FIGURES
Costs*

$$
\begin{aligned}
X &= 23.5 \text{ cents} \times A = 10 = \$2.35 \\
Y &= 16.9 \text{ cents} \times B = 6 = 1.014 \\
Z &= 7.9 \text{ cents} \times C = 4 = \underline{.316} \\
& \qquad\qquad\qquad\qquad\qquad \$3.68
\end{aligned}
$$

= value of Basic Materials per 100 lbs. of 10:6:4 blend or $1.84 per 50 lb. bag.

*Salt Lake City—Fall 1966, List

Now add to this the cost or savings made in handling and storing, as well as the convenience and waste factors in the actual use and application. If your material has acceptable and guaranteed quantities of iron and other trace elements, add approximately 75 cents/50 lb. bag to its value as well.

Do not be misled by exaggerated "coverage" claims.
Anyone can spread their product on thinner and cover more ground—
and let the plants starve!

FERTILIZERS AND SOIL ADDITIVES

FERTILIZATION

Amount of mixed material necessary to apply one pound of actual nitrogen
per each one thousand square surface feet (1 lb./1,000 sq. ft.)
(expressed in pounds per thousand, pounds per acre, and acres per ton).

Percentage of N in Mix	Pounds of Mix for 1 lb. Act. N per 1,000 sq. ft.	Pounds of Mix for 1 lb. Act. N per 1,000 sq. ft. on Acre Basis	Equiv. Tons per Acre	Approx. Acreage Covered per Ton
1	100	4356	2.178	.46
2	50	2178	1.096	.92
3	33.3	1452	.726	1.38
4	25	1089	.544	1.84
5	20	871	.435	2.30
6	16.6	726	.363	2.75
7	14.3	622	.311	3.21
8	12.5	545	.273	3.66
9	11.1	484	.242	4.13
10	10	436	.218	4.58
11	9	400	.200	5.04
12	8.3	363	.182	5.50
14	7.1	311	.155	6.45
16	6.25	272	.136	7.35
18	5.5	242	.121	8.26
20	5	218	.109	9.17
22	4.5	198	.099	10.10
24	4.1	181	.091	11.00
26	3.8	168	.094	11.90
28	3.5	156	.078	12.80
30	3.3	145	.073	13.70
32	3.1	136	.068	14.70
34	3	128	.064	15.60
36	2.75	121	.061	16.40
38	2.6	115	.058	17.20
40	2.5	109	.055	18.10
42	2.4	104	.052	19.20
44	2.27	100	.050	20.00
46	2.17	95	.048	20.80
48	2.1	91	.045	22.20
50	2	87	.044	22.70

Example: If a 16-16-8 mix is to be used, and 3 lbs. actual Nitrogen is required; from the chart:
6.25 lbs. of the mix is required for 1 lb. act. N; per 1,000 sq. ft. 6.25 x 3 = 18.75 lbs.
material required for 3 lbs. actual N. On an acreage basis this would be 3 x 136 = .408 Tons.

FERTILIZERS AND SOIL ADDITIVES

STEER MANURE
Rates Per Acre Based on Required Rates per Thousand Sq. Ft.

Rate Per 1,000 Sq. Ft.	Equivalent Rate Per Acre
1.0 Cubic Yards	43.56 Cubic Yards
1.5	65.34
2.0	87.12
2.5	108.90
3.0	130.68
3.5	152.46
4.0	174.24
4.5	196.02
5.0	217.80

Example: 3 Cu. Yds. required per 1,000 sq. ft. = 3 x 43.56 = 130.68 cu. yds./acre.

STEER MANURE
Coverage: Depth in Inches Per Square Surface Footage

One Sack (2.5 Cu. Ft.) Will Cover:		One Sack (2.0 Cu. Ft.) Will Cover:	
Depth Inches	Coverage Square Feet	Depth Inches	Coverage Square Feet
.25″	120.0 sq. ft.	.25″	96.0 sq. ft.
50″	60.0 sq. ft.	.50″	48.0 sq. ft.
1.00″	30.0 sq. ft.	1.00″	24.0 sq. ft.
2.00″	15.0 sq. ft.	2.00″	12.0 sq. ft.
3.00″	10.0 sq. ft.	3.00″	8.0 sq. ft.
4.00″	7.5 sq. ft.	4.00″	6.0 sq. ft.
6.00″	5.0 sq. ft.	6.00″	4.0 sq. ft.
12.00″	2.5 sq. ft.	12.00″	2.0 sq. ft.

STRAW
Coverage Per Bale: Depth in Inches Per Square Surface Footage

One Bale (Assuming 16.6 Cu. Ft./Bale) Will Cover:	
1.00″ Deep	200 Sq. Ft.
2.00″	100
4.00″	50
8.00″	25
12.00″	16.6

FERTILIZERS AND SOIL ADDITIVES

FERTILIZER
WHAT'S IT WORTH?

Confused with "Formula", "Ratio", "Rate", "Use", "Demands", and other
emotional and semi-scientific terms?

Check these tables to find real comparisons and values.

CHART NO. 1
POUNDS OF ACTUAL NUTRIENTS PER (N or P_2O_5 or K_2O)

Check the left-hand column against the fertilizer package formula,
read across to the right to find actual quantity of specific nutrient in bag (top row)
of either N, P_2O_5 or K_2O.

When Nutrient Formula % Is	25 lb. Bag	40 lb. Bag	50 lb. Bag	80 lb. Bag	100 lb. Bag
1%	0.25	0.4	0.5	0.8	1.0
3%	0.7	1.2	1.5	2.4	3.0
4%	1.0	1.6	2.0	3.2	4.0
5%	1.25	2.0	2.5	4.0	5.0
6%	1.5	2.4	3.0	4.8	6.0
10%	2.5	4.0	5.0	8.0	10.0
16%	4.0	6.4	8.0	12.8	16.0
21%	5.25	8.4	10.5	16.8	21.0
22%	5.5	8.8	11.0	17.6	22.0
24%	6.0	9.6	12.0	19.2	24.0
34%	8.5	13.6	17.0	27.2	34.0
44%	11.0	17.6	22.0	35.2	44.0
60%	15.0	24.0	30.0	48.0	60.0

ORGANIC MATERIALS USEFUL AS FERTILIZERS

Animal product	Average % Nitrogen N	Average % Phosphoric Acid K	Average % Potash P	Speed of Availability
Dried Blood				
Dried Blood	12	0	0	moderate
Tankage	8 - 10	5 - 12	0	moderate
Steamed Bonemeal	1 - 2	22 - 30	0	slow
Bone Tankage	6	30	0	moderate
Fish Meal	8 - 10	5	0	moderate
Sheep Manure	2 - 3	1 - 2	1 - 2	slow
Poultry Manure	2 - 3	1	1 - 2	slow
Vegetable Product				
Cotton Seed Meal	8	2	2	slow
Hard Wood Ash	0	2	8	slow
Soft Wood Ash	0	2	4	slow
Linseed Meal	5	2	2	slow
Soybean Meal	6	3	1	slow

MANUFACTURED FERTILIZER CHEMICALS*

Chemical	Average % Nitrogen N	Average % Phosphoric Acid K	Average % Potash P	Speed of Availability	Reaction
Ammonium Chloride (Muriate of Ammonium)	26	26	0	quick	acid
Ammonium Sulfate	20	0	0	quick	very acid
Ammonium Nitrate	35	0	0	quick	acid
Sodium Nitrate (Nitrate of Soda)	16	0	0	very quick	alkaline
Potassium Chloride (Muriate of Potash)	0	0	50	quick	neutral
Potassium Phosphate	0	15	40	quick	neutral
Potassium Nitrate	12	0	40	quick	slightly acid
Rock Phosphate	0	25	0	slow	alkaline
Potassium Sulfate	0	0	50	quick	neutral
Superphosphate	0	20	0	slow	neutral
Mono-Ammonium Phosphate	12	60	0	quick	acid
Di-Ammonium Phosphate	20	53	0	quick	alkaline

*None of these is a complete fertilizer, supplying more or less balanced amounts of nitrogen, phosphate and potash. But they are useful where just one fertilizer element is lacking in the soil (in some cases, two), and for compounding fertilizer mixtures.

APPROXIMATE AMOUNT OF SPRAY MATERIAL REQUIRED
FOR TREES OF DIFFERENT SIZES

Height in Feet	Spread in Feet	Gallons Per Application
4	3	up to ½
5	6	3
6	8	4
7	10	5
8	12	6
9	14	7
10	16	8
11	18	10
13	20	12
16	24	13
19	26	14
25	30	15
30	35	20
35*	38	25

*Trees above the height of 30-35 feet are best sprayed by a commercial arborist with a high-pressure sprayer. Trees sprayed early in the season require only about 1/3 of the spray needed in full leaf.

FERTILIZERS AND SOIL ADDITIVES

COMMERCIAL LIQUID FERTILIZERS FOR FOLIAR FERTILIZING*

Trade name	% Nitrogen N	% Phosphoric Acid K	% Potash P
DuPont Foliar Fertilizer	19	22	16
Folium	20	20	20
Instant Vigoro	19	28	14
Orthogrow	10	5	5
Ra-Pid-Gro	23	21	17

*Never apply undiluted to plants but mix with water according to manufacturer's instructions and apply as directed on the label.

PLANT MATERIALS

SEEDED GRASSES – RATE AND TIME OF SEEDING

Grass	Pounds of Seed per 1,000 sq ft	Time of Seeding	Germination Time (Days) Beginning-Full
Bahiagrass (Pasapalum notatum)	2-3	Spring	7-28
Bermudagrass (Cynodon dactylon)	2-3	Spring	7-21
Blue gramagrass, unhulled (Boutelous gracilis)	1-1½	Spring	7-28
Buffalograss (Buchloe dactyloides)	½-1	Spring	7-28
Canada bluegrass (Poa compressa)	2-3	Fall	10-28
Carpetgrass (Axonopus compressus)	3-4	Spring	10-21
Centidedegrass (Eremochloa ephiruroides)	2-3	Spring	- -
Chewings fescue (Festuca rubra commutata)	3-5	Fall	7-21
Colonial bentgrass (Agrostis tenuis 'Highland' and 'Astoria'	1-2	Fall	7-28
Creeping bentgrass (Agrostis polustris 'Seaside')	1-2	Fall	7-28
Crested wheatgrass (Agropyron cristatum)	1-2	Fall	5-14
Japanese lawngrass, hulled (Zoysia japonica)	1-2	Spring	10-28
Kentucky bluegrass, common (Poa pratensis)	2-3	Fall	10-28
Merion bluegrass (Poa pratensis 'Merion')	1-2	Fall	1-28
Red fescue (Festuca rubra)	3-5	Fall	7-2
Redtop (Agrostis alba)	1-2	Fall	5-10
Rough bluegrass (Poa trivialis)	3-5	Fall	7-21
Ryegrass, domestic or annual (Lolium multiflorum)	4-6	Spring-Fall	5-14
Ryegrass, perennial (Lolium perenne)	4-6	Spring-Fall	5-14
Tall fescue (Festuca arundinacae 'Alta' and 'Ky. 3l')	4-6	Fall	5-14
Velvet bluegrass (Agrostis canina)	1-2	Fall	7-21
Mixture for sunny areas: 75% bluegrass, 25% red fescue	2-4	Fall	- -
Mixture for shady areas: 25% bluegrass, 75% red fescue	2-4	Fall	- -

*Courtesy - U. S. Department of Agriculture

VEGETATIVE GRASSES — RATE AND TIME OF PLANTING

Grass	Amount of Planting Material Per 1,000 Sq. Ft.	Time of Planting
Bermudagrass (Cynodon dactylon)	10 square feet of nursery sod or 1 bushel of stolons.	Spring-summer
Buffalograss (Buchloe dactyloides)	25-50 square feet of sod	Spring
Carpetgrass (Axonopus compressus)	8-10 square feet of sod	Spring-summer
Centipedegrass (Eremochloa ephiruroides)	8-10 square feet of sod	Spring-summer
Creeping bentgrass (Agrostis polustris 'Seaside')	80-100 square feet of nursery sod or 10 bushels of stolons	Fall
Velvet bentgrass (Agrostis canina)	80-100 square feet of nursery sod or 10 bushels of stolons	Fall
Japanese lawngrass, hulled (Zoysia japonica)	30 square feet of sod when plugging 6 square feet of sod when sprigging	Spring-summer

*Courtesy — U.S. Department of Agriculture

AREA MEASUREMENTS
100 Plants Spaced x' Requires y Sq. Ft.

Spacing	Area	
9'' O.C.	46 Sq. Ft.	6.75^2
1' 0'' O.C.	81 Sq. Ft.	9.0^2
1' 6'' O.C.	182 Sq. Ft.	13.5^2
2' 0'' O.C.	324 Sq. Ft.	18.0^2
2' 6'' O.C.	506 Sq. Ft.	22.5^2
3' 0'' O.C.	729 Sq. Ft.	27.0^2
3' 6'' O.C.	991 Sq. Ft.	31.5^2
4' 0'' O.C.	1,296 Sq. Ft.	36.0^2
4' 6'' O.C.	1,640 Sq. Ft.	40.5^2
5' 0'' O.C.	2.024 Sq. Ft.	45.0^2
6' 0'' O.C.	2,916 Sq. Ft.	54.0^2
7' 0'' O.C.	3,964 Sq. Ft.	63.0^2
8' 0'' O.C.	5,184 Sq. Ft.	72.0^2
9' 0'' O.C.	6,560 Sq. Ft.	81.0^2
10' 0'' O.C.	8,096 Sq. Ft.	90.0^2
15' 0'' O.C.	18,225 Sq. Ft.	135.0^2
20' 0'' O.C.	32,384 Sq. Ft.	180.0^2
25' 0'' O.C.	50,625 Sq. Ft.	225.0^2
30' 0'' O.C.	72,900 Sq. Ft.	270.0^2
35' 0'' O.C.	99,225 Sq. Ft.	315.0^2
40' 0'' O.C.	129,536 Sq. Ft.	360.0^2

BEDDING PLANT GUIDE & SEEDING CHART

COLOR:

R — red	Ro — rose	Y — yellow	M — maroon	Cr — crimson
P — pink	Bu — buff	O — orange	S — salmon	Sc — scarlet
B — blue	W — white	V — violet	Co — copper	L — lavender
				Mah — mahogany

BLOOM TIME: May — 5,   June — 6,   July — 7,   etc.

GERMINATION: Days required under good growing conditions.

TIME TO PLANT: F1   In flats one month before plant out time.

F 2   In flats two months before plant out time.

F3   In flats three months before plant out time.

++ May repeat with successive plantings.

May — April — Fall — etc.   Plant seeds outside
in month prescribed.

NOTE: Such plants as Coleus, geraniums, etc., are carried over from/or as cuttings and space prohibits treatment of these plants.

SHADE TREE PLANTING CHART

Bare Root (Actual Planting on Job)		
Size	Prepared Beds	Spade, etc.
6-8'	.7 hr.	1.0 hr.
8-10'	.8 hr.	1.2 hrs.
10-12'	.9 hr.	1.3 hrs.
1 ½-2''	1.0 hr.	1.5 hrs.
2-2 ½''	1.3 hrs.	2.0 hrs.
2 ½-3''	1.5 hrs.	2.5 hrs.
3-4''	2.5 hrs.	3.7 hrs.
Etc.		

Balled & Burlapped (Actual Planting on Jobs)		
Size	Prepared Beds	Spade, etc.
6-8'	1.2 hrs.	1.7 hrs.
8-10'	1.5 hrs.	2.2 hrs.
10-12'	2.0 hrs.	2.8 hrs.
1 ½-2''	2.5 hrs.	3.3 hrs.
2-2 ½''	3.5 hrs.	4.5 hrs.
2 ½-3''	5.0 hrs.	6.0 hrs.
3-4''	7.0 hrs.	8.5 hrs.
Etc.		

It should be noted here that all man-hour charts indicate actual time spent on the proper planting of the material on the job. To refer back to the percentages for travel time, the charts might be made more readily usable if the charts were broken down with the percentage of travel time included in each case. Codes could be used for office workers, so estimates could be made under "A", "B", "C", etc., in whichever travel time area that the job might fall under.

BEDDING PLANT CHART

ONE FOOT AND UNDER

Proper Name of Flower Common Name	Height Inches	Colors	Space Inches	Bloom Time	Days to Germinate	Time to Sow
Ageratum houstonianum Flossflower	8-12	LBWP	8	7-8-9-10	14	F-3
Arcototis stoechadifolia African daisy.	10-12	WYPMLCrO	24	7-8-9-10	21	F-3
Brachycome iberidifolia Swan River Daisy	9-12	BRoWV	10	7-8-9	10	F-2
Coreopsis drummondi Calliopsis.	9-36	YMah	15	6-7-8-9-10	14	F-1
Dimorphotheca aurantiaca Cape marigold	12	WYOS	10	7-8-9	15-21	F-2
Impatiens balsamina Garden balsam.	3-30	WLPR	24	8-9	15	F-2
Lobelia erinus Edging lobelia	4-10	BR	8	7-8-9-10	10-15	F-3
Lobularia maritima Sweet alyssum	4-8	WV	8	5-6-7-8-9-10	10-20	Apr.⧸⧸ F-2
Myosotis alpertris Forget-me-not	12	WRoB	10	5-6-7-8-9-10	14	F-3
Nierembergia hippomanica Dwarf cupflower	6	LBV	10	7-8-9-10		F-3
Petunia hybrida Common petunia.	10-18	PSRoWLV	12	7-8-9-10	10	F-3
Portulaca grandiflora Rose moss	4-6	PRSCrWYO	10	7-8-9-10	14	F-2
Sanvitalia procumbens Creeping zinnia	6-10	Y	12	6-7-8-9-10	10	F-3
Tagetes patula French marigold	8-15	YOMah	15	6-7-8-9-10	8	F-1

BEDDING PLANT CHART

ONE FOOT AND UNDER (CONTINUED)

Proper Name of Flower Common Name	Height Inches	Colors	Space Inches	Bloom Time	Days to Germinate	Time to Sow
Tropaeolum minus Dwarf nasturtium	12	ScOYR	15	6-7-8-9-10	12-14q	May
Verbena hybrida Garden verbena	8-18	WPRoSLV	18	7-8-9-10	14	F-2
Zinnia elegans Common zinnia	12-36	WYOPRo	8-18	7-8-9-10	5-10	F-1

BEDDING PLANT CHART

ONE FOOT TO TWO FEET (CONTINUED)

Proper Name of Flower Common Name	Height Inches	Colors	Space Inches	Bloom Time	Days to Germinate	Time to Sow
Gypsophila elegans Baby's breath	12-15	WPRo	6	7-8-9 ·	10-14	F-1
Helipterum roseum Rose spray.	15	WPRo	15	7-8	14	F-2
Iberis umbellata Candytuft	12-18	WPLRo	12	6-7-8-9-10	14	F-1
Impatiens balsamina Garden balsam.	3-30	WLPR	24	8-9	15	F-2
Linum grandiflorum Flowering flax	15-18	Cr	6	5-6-7-8-9-10	14	F-2
Lupinus pubescens Annual lupine	12-14	BRoW	12	7-8	10	F-2
Mathiola incana Annual stock.	15-30	WPLCrV	15	7-8-9	6-10	F-2
Nicotiana alata Winged tobacco.	15-30	WPCr	24	6-7-8-9-10	10	F-3
Nigella damascena Love-in-a-mist	18	WB	18	7-8-9	14	Fall-Apr.
Phlox drummondi Drummond phlox	10-20	WYBuSCrVP	18	7-8-9	10-15	F-2
Reseda ororata Mignonette	12-18	YCoCrW	18	7-8-9-10	11-14	F-2
Salvia splendens Scarlet sage	10-24	Sc	24	8-9-10	14	F-3
Trachymene coerulea Blue laceflower	18-30	LB	15	7-8-9-10	12-14	F-2
Zinnia elegans Common zinnia.	12-36	WYOPRo	8-18	7-8-9-10	5-10	F-1

BEDDING PLANT CHART

ONE FOOT TO TWO FEET

Proper Name of Flower / Common Name	Height Inches	Colors	Space Inches	Bloom Time	Days to Germinate	Time to Sow
Anchusa capensis / Cape bugloss	18	B	10	7-8-9-10		F-2
Antirrhinum majus / Snapdragon	12-36	WYPCoCr	15	7-8-9-10	10-14	F-3
Browallia speciosa / Amethyst	10-18	BW	10	6-7-8-9-10	28-40	F-2
Calendula officinalis / Pot Marigold	15-24	BuYORo	15	7-8-9-10	14	F-1
Callistephus chinensis / China aster	18-36	WPRoLV	15-24	7-8-9-10	8-12	F-2
Celosia eristata / Crested cockscomb	10-18	YOCrVR	24	7-8-9	6-10	F-2
Celosia plumosa / Feather cockscomb	12-36	YORCr	24	7-8-9	6-10	F-2
Centaurea imperialis / Sweet sultan	18-30	WPYRoL	20	7-8-9	15	F-2
Chrysanthemum coronarium / Crown daisy	18	WYPCr	15	7-8-9	11-18	F-2
Coreopsis drummondi / Calliopsis.	9-36	YMah	15	6-7-8-9-10	14	F-1
Dianthus caryophyllus / Carnation	15-18	PRWYS	12	6-7-8-9-10	10	F-3
Erysimum perofskianum / Annual wallflower.	12-24	YMah	12	8-9-10	10-14	F-2
Eschscholtzia californica / California poppy	15-18	WYOSRo	12	6-7-8	10	F-2
Gaillardia pulchella / Rosering gaillardia.	15-24	YOM	15	6-7-8-9-10	15-20	F-2
Godetia grandiflora / Satinflower	12-20	RoLWPCr	12	6-7-8-9-10	15	F-2
Gomphrena globosa / Globe amaranth.	18-24	WPCr	12	7-8-9	15	F-2

PLANT MATERIALS

BEDDING PLANT CHART

TWO FEET AND OVER

Proper Name of Flower Common Name	Height Inches	Colors	Space Inches	Bloom Time	Days to Germinate	Time to Sow
Centaurea americana Basket flower	36	WLP	20	7-8-9	20-30	May or F-2
Centaurea cayanus Cornflower	24-30	WBVCrMP	24	6-7-8-9	15	F-2
Clarkia elegans Rose clarkia.	24	WPRoSL	18	7-8-9-10	14	April
Cleome spinosa Spiderflower	36-48	PY	15	7-8-9	21	F-2
Coreopsis drummondi Calliopsis.	9-36	YMah	15	6-7-8-9-10	14	F-1
Cosmos bipinnatus Cosmos	36-60	RoPW	24	7-8-9-10	10-14	F-1
Cosmos sulphureus Yellow cosmos	36-48	YO	24	8-9-10	14	F-2
Cynoglossum amabile Chinese forget-me-not . .	30	BW	12	6-7-8	10	F-2
Delphinium ajacis Rocket larkspur.	36-48	PWRoLV	15	7-8-9	20-28	
Helichrysum bracteatum Strawflower.	30	WPYOCrRo	30	8-9	14	F-2
Hunnemannia fumariaefolia Santa Barbara poppy. . .	24	Y	15	7-8-9-10	14	F-2
Lavatera trimestris Herb tree mallow.	24-36	PW	15	7-8-9-10	14-35	F-2
Limonium sinuatum Notchleaf sea lavender. .	34-30	WYRoBL	10	7-8-9	14-21	F-2
Papaver rhoeas Shirley poppy	36-48	WPRoSSC	15	6-7-8	10-14	Apr.,May
Papaver somniferum Opium poppy	36-48	WPRoCr	20	7-8	10-14	Apr.,May

BEDDING PLANT CHART

TWO FEET AND OVER (CONTINUED)

Proper Name of Flower Common Name	Height Inches	Colors	Space Inches	Bloom Time	Days to Germinate	Time to Sow
Salpiglossis sinuata Painted tongue	30	YVLCrW	18	7-8-9-10	14	F-3
Salvia farinacea Meallycup sage	30	B	18	7-8-9-10	15-20	F-3
Scabiosa atropurpurea Pincushion flower	24-36	WLPMRo	18	7-8-9-10	14-21	F-3
Tagetes erecta African marigold	24-36	YO	20	7-8-9-10	8	F-1
Tithonia rotundifolia Mexican sunflower	72	Ro	30	9-10	25	F-3
Zinnea elegans Common zinnia.	12-36	WYOPRo	8-18	7-8-9-10	5-10	F-1

BEDDING PLANT CHART — VINES

Proper Name of Flower Common Name	Height Inches	Colors	Space Inches	Bloom Time	Days to Germinate	Time to Sow
Cobaca scandens Purplebell . . . . Vine		BV	8	7-8-9	15-20	F-2
Ipomoea purpurea Garden morning-glory . . . Vine		WPRoB	6	7-8-9-10	10	Apr.,May
Lathyrus odoratus Sweet pea . . . . Vine		WPRoBVLS	6	6-7-8-9	10	Feb., Mar.
Phascolus coccineus Scarlet runner bean . . . . . Vine		Sc.	8	7-8-9	7-10	F-3
Thunbergia rotundifolia Black-eyed clockvine. . . . Vine		WYBuO	8	7-8-9	21	F-2

CHARACTERISTICS OF SOME TURF GRASSES

Grass	Purity (%)	Germi nation (%)	Germi- nation Period Days	Seed/Lb. in Millions
Agrostis Alba (Red Top)	92	90	6 - 10	5.0
Agrostis Palustris (Creeping Bent)	95	90	7 - 14	8.0
Agrostis Tenuis (Colonial Bent)	95	90	7 - 14	8.5
Cynodon Dactylon (Bermuda Grass)	97	85	14 - 21	1.8
Festuca Elatior (Meadow Fescue)	95	90	6 - 10	0.23
Var. Arundinacease Tall (Tall Fescue)	95	90	7 - 14	0.23
Festuca Rubra (Red Fescue)	95	80	7 - 14	0.615
Lolium Domesticum (Domestic Ryegrass)	98	90	5 - 10	.23
Lolium Perenne (Perennial Ryegrass)	98	90	5 - 10	.23
Poa Pratensis (Kentucky Bluegrass)	85	80	10 - 20	2.2
Poa Trivialis (Roughstalk Blue)	85	80	10 - 20	2.5
Dichondra Repens* (Dichondra)	96	90	7 - 14	.8
Trifolium Repens* (White Clover)	96	95	5 - 10	.7

*Not grass but often used as turf.

AREA REQUIRED FOR GROUND COVERS
SQUARE FEET PER FLAT

Spacing in Inches O.C.	Plants per Flat			
	50	64	81	100
4	5.56	7.11	9.00	11.11
6	12.50	16.00	20.25	25.00
8	22.22	28.44	·36.00	44.44
9	28.12	36.00	45.56	56.25
10	34.72	44.44	56.25	69.44
12	50.00	64.00	81.00	100.00
16	88.89	113.77	144.00	177.77
18	112.50	144.00	182.25	225.00
24	200.00	256.00	324.00	400.00
30	312.50	400.00	506.25	625.00

FLATS OF PLANTS REQUIRED PER ONE HUNDRED SQUARE FEET
VARIOUS SPACINGS/VARIOUS QUANTITIES PER FLAT

Spacing in Inches O.C.	Quantities of Plants per Flat			
	50	64	81	100
4	18.00	14.06	11.11	9.00
6	8.00	6.25	4.94	4.00
8	4.50	3.51	2.78	2.25
9	3.55	2.78	2.20	1.78
10	2.88	2.25	1.78	1.44
12	2.00	1.56	1.23	1.00
16	1.12	0.87	0.69	0.56
18	0.90	0.70	0.56	0.45
24	0.50	0.39	0.31	0.25
30	0.32	0.25	0.20	0.16

GRASS SEED
RECOMMENDED SEEDING RATES

Grass	Seed/Lb. in Millions	Rate in Lbs. Per 1,000 Sq. Ft.	Rate in Lbs. Per Acre
Agrostis Alba (Red Top)	5.0	1	44
Agrostis Palustris (Creeping Bentgrass)	8.0	1	44
Agrostis Tenuis (Colonial Bentgrass)	8.5	1	44
Cynodon Dactylon (Bermudagrass)	1.8	2	88
Festuca Elatior (Meadow Fescue)	.23	6	264
Var. Arundinacease Tall (Tall Fescue)	.23	6	264
Festuca Rubra (Red Fescue)	.615	4	176
Lolium Domesticum (Domestic Rye)	.23	8	352
Lolium Perenne (Perennial Rye)	.23	8	352
Poa Pratensis (Kentucky Bluegrass)	2.2	2	88
Poa Trivialis (Roughstalk Blue)	2.5	2	88
Dichondra Repens* (Dichondra)	0.8	1	44
Trifolium Repens* (White Clover)	0.7	2	88

*Not grasses but often used as turf.

TURF AND OTHER GROUND COVERS VIA PLUGS
PLUGS PER FLAT* AND SQUARE FOOT COVERAGE
VARIOUS PLUG SIZES AND VARIOUS PLUG SPACINGS

Plug Size Sq. Inches	Plugs Per Flat	Sq. Ft. Coverages per Spacings Indicated		
		6″ O.C.	9″ O.C.	12″ O.C.
1.25	200	50	110	200
1.00	280	70	160	280
0.75	500	125	280	500
0.50	1,100	280	625	1,100

*Normal size flat. Example: Plan calls for one square inch plugs 9″ O.C. If area is 4,500 square feet, from the chart find that one flat will cover 160 square feet 9″ O.C. Therefore, 4,500 ÷ 160 = 28 flats needed.

PLANTS REQUIRED PER ONE HUNDRED SQUARE FEET
VARIOUS SPACINGS

Spacing in Inches O.C.	Plants per 100 Square Feet	Spacing in Inches O.C.	Plants per 100 Square Feet
4	900.00	18	45.00
6	400.00	24	25.00
8	225.00	30	16.00
9	178.00	36	11.11
10	144.00	48	6.25
12	100.00	72	2.78
16	56.00		

NURSERY CONTAINER STOCK

Approximate Weights and Plant-Ball Volume		
Container	Approx. Weight in Pounds	Volume in Cubic Feet
1 gallon	7	0.15
5 gallon	40	0.60
15 gallon	188	2.00
16" Box	235	2.50
20" Box	510	4.75
24" Box	725	6.70
30" Box	1,500	13.60
36" Box	2,500	23.40
42" Box	3,700	31.70
48" Box	6,000	40.30
54" Box	7,000	56.00
60" Box	8,000	74.40

TREE PIT EXCAVATION FOR NURSERY CONTAINER STOCK
SQUARE PITS/VERTICAL SIDES

Container	Pit: L	W	D	Soil Volume Displacement in Cu. Ft.*
1 gallon	10" x	10" x	12"	.7
5 gallon	18" x	18" x	20"	3.7
15 gallon	30" x	30" x	24"	12.5
16" Box	32" x	32" x	24"	14.2
20" Box	40" x	40" x	24"	22.2
24" Box	48" x	48" x	24"	32.0
30" Box	54" x	54" x	27"	45.5
36" Box	66" x	66" x	32"	80.6
42" Box	78" x	78" x	32"	112.7
48" Box	90" x	90" x	36"	168.7
54" Box	102" x	102" x	36"	216.7
60" Box	108" x	108" x	42"	283.5

*Swellage Factor not applied. See Table for swellage, various soil types.

LINERS AND HEDGE PLANTS
PLANTS REQUIRED PER ONE HUNDRED LINEAL FEET

Spacing (in Feet)	No. Required per 100 Lin. Ft.
0.33	300.0
0.50	200.0
0.67	150.0
1.00	100.0
1.50	66.7
2.00	50.0
2.50	40.0
3.00	33.3
3.50	28.6
4.00	25.0
4.50	22.3
5.00	20.0
6.00	16.7
6.50	15.4
7.00	14.3
7.50	13.3
8.00	12.5
8.50	11.8
9.00	11.1
9.50	10.5
10.00	10.0

Example: If plants were required for one mile of screening at 8 ft. spacings, from the chart find that 12.5 per 100 ft. x 52.8 = 660 plants per mile.

NUMBER OF SHRUBS OR PLANTS FOR AN ACRE

Distance Apart	No. of Plants	Distance Apart	No. of Plants	Distance Apart	No. of Plants
3 x 3 Inches	696,690	4 x 4 Feet	2,722	13 x 13 Feet	257
4 x 4 Inches	392,040	4½ x 4½ Feet	2,151	14 x 14 Feet	222
6 x 6 Inches	174,240	5 x 1 Feet	8,712	15 x 15 Feet	193
9 x 9 Inches	77,440	5 x 2 Feet	4,356	16 x 16 Feet	170
1 x 1 Foot	43,560	5 x 3 Feet	2,904	16½ x 16½ Feet	160
1½ x 1½ Feet	19,360	5 x 4 Feet	3,178	17 x 17 Feet	150
2 x 1 Feet	21,780	5 x 5 Feet	1,742	18 x 18 Feet	134
2 x 2 Feet	10,890	5½ x 5½ Feet	1,417	19 x 19 Feet	120
2½ x 2½ Feet	6,980	6 x 6 Feet	1,210	20 x 20 Feet	108
3 x 1 Feet	14,620	6½ x 6½ Feet	1,031	25 x 25 Feet	69
3 x 2 Feet	7,260	7 x 7 Feet	881	30 x 30 Feet	48
3 x 3 Feet	4,840	8 x 8 Feet	680	33 x 33 Feet	40
3½ x 3½ Feet	3,555	9 x 9 Feet	537	40 x 40 Feet	27
4 x 1 Feet	10,890	10 x 10 Feet	435	50 x 50 Feet	17
4 x 2 Feet	5,445	11 x 11 Feet	360	60 x 60 Feet	12
4 x 3 Feet	3,630	12 x 12 Feet	302	66 x 66 Feet	10

REQUIREMENTS OF POPULAR ANNUALS

Name	Sun/Shade	Height	Spacing
Ageratum	Sun	6 - 10''	10 - 12''
Alyssum	Sun	4 - 8''	10 - 12''
Aster			
Tall	Sun	12 - 24''	12 - 18''
Dwarf	Sun	8 - 12''	8 - 12''
Cockscomb	Sun	16 - 40''	10 - 24''
Coleus	P.S./Shade	18''	12 - 14''
Dahlia	Sun	12 - 40''	12 - 18''
Impatiens	Shade/P.S.	6 - 14''	8 - 12''
Marigold			
Dwarf	Sun	6 - 10''	10 - 12''
Medium	Sun	12 - 18''	12 - 14''
Tall	Sun	20 - 36''	18 - 24''
Pansy	Sun/P.S.	6 - 10''	6 - 8''
Petunia	Sun	12 - 18''	12 - 14''
Phlox	Sun	4 - 12''	6 - 8''
Portulaca	Sun	4 - 6''	10 - 12''
Salvia	Sun/P.S.	12 - 36''	12 - 18''
Snapdragon	Sun/P.S.	6 - 36''	12 - 18''
Verbena	Sun	6 - 12''	12 - 18''
Zinnia			
Tall	Sun	18 - 36''	12 - 24''
Dwarf	Sun	6 - 14''	10''

GRASS STOLONS: QUANTITIES REQUIRED FOR BROADCAST DISTRIBUTION

Grass	Bushel Rate Per 1,000 Sq. Ft.*	Bushel Rate Per Acre*
St. Augustine	5.0	220
Hybrid Bermuda	2.0 to 4.0	88 to 176
Bentgrass	4.0 to 6.0	176 to 264

*Soil conditions, season, quality of expected maintenance and initial cost influence rate of stolonization desirable. Desirable establishment is also a major factor.

GRASS STOLONS: DISTRIBUTION RATE BY MEANS OF SPRIGGING

Spacings Sq. Inches	Bushels Required Per Spacing	
	Per 1,000 Square Feet	Per Acre
6" O.C.	2.0 Bu.	88 Bu.
9" O.C.	1.25 Bu.	55 Bu.
12" O.C.	.5 Bu.	22 Bu.

PLANT COST PER COLOR DAY

The accompanying table contains the information used to determine color costs and shows the comparative costs to produce plantings of five plants used by the Dallas Parks Department.

The figures include all initial costs for plant bed preparation and other costs involved in starting a new planting. Subsequent planting and maintenance costs would be lower, so in succeeding years the cost per color day would be reduced. This would be particularly true for a permanent shrub planting such as azaleas or a planting of cannas which in Dallas would need to be divided and replanted only about every three years.

This approach to park planting has helped not only in standardizing the number of different plants grown, but has aided in determining the approximate cost of each planting. From this the relative worth of a plant or planting in color production can easily be determined.

PLANT COLOR COST PER 1,000 SQUARE FEET

	No. of Plants	Spacing O.C.	Plant Cost	Planting Maint.	No. Days of Color	No. Days of Care	Total Cost	Cost Per Color Day
Cannas	99	3'	$ 7	$286	185	240	$ 293	$ 1.58
Lantana	396	1.5'	$ 48	$278	185	215	$ 326	$ 1.76
Acalypha	396	1.5'	$ 55	$280	185	185	$3,335	$ 1,81
Petunia	553	1.5'	$ 44	$234	70	90	$ 278	$ 3.97
Zinnia			$ 1	$217	50	95	$ 218	$ 4.36
Azalea	200		$198	$863	18	365	$1,061	$58.94

PLANT COSTS AND COVERAGES

Dichondra
(Cut out 64 squares per flat)
8 rows spaced 4" apart will cover 7 sq. ft.
8 rows spaced 6" apart will cover 16 sq. ft.
8 rows spaced 8" apart will cover 28 sq. ft.
8 rows spaced 10" apart will cover 44 sq. ft.
8 rows spaced 12" apart will cover 64 sq. ft.
These spaces are figured center to center.

PLANTING OPERATIONS

Ground Covers
(Cut out, place and plant; soil already prepared)
45 minutes per flat.

Dichondra
(Soil already prepared)
30 minutes per flat.

COVERAGES

Ground Covers
(100 plants per flat)
Spaced 4" apart will cover 11 sq. ft.
Spaced 6" apart will cover 25 sq. ft.
Spaced 8" apart will cover 44 sq. ft.
Spaced 10" apart will cover 70 sq. ft.
Spaced 12" apart will cover 100 sq. ft.
Spaced 15" apart will cover 156 sq. ft.
Spaced 18" apart will cover 225 sq. ft.
Spaced 24" apart will cover 400 sq. ft.
Spacing is figured center to center.

Redwood Paving and Dichondra
Figure ¾ of area in redwood and ¼ in Dichondra.
EXAMPLE: 100 sq. ft. to be paved will require 75 sq. ft. redwood blocks and ½ flat Dichondra.

LAWN WORK

Seed Coverages

1 lb. clover will cover 250 sq. ft.
1 lb. Bluegrass will cover 150 sq. ft.
1 lb. mixed seed will cover 175 sq. ft.
1 lb. Rye will cover 100 sq. ft.

1 lb. Dichondra will cover 4,000 sq. ft.
1 lb. Chewings Fescue will cover 100 sq. ft.
1 lb. Astoria Bent will cover 250 sq. ft.
1 lb. Seaside Bent will cover 300 sq. ft.

ESTIMATING PLANTS PER LINEAL FOOT OF HEDGE

Plant Spacing	Plants per Lineal Foot	Plants per 10 Lineal Feet
10"	1.2	12.0
12"	1.0	10.0
15"	.8	8.0
18"	.67	6.7
24"	.5	5.0
30"	.4	4.0
3'	.33	3.3
4'	.25	2.5
5'	.2	2.0

SUGGESTED HEDGE PLANTING SPACING *

Type of Hedge	Suggested Spacing
Berberis thunbergi and other Barberry	15 in. apart
Buxus suffruticosa	12 in. apart
Euonymus alatus and compactus	18 in. apart
Ilex crenata varieties	24 in. apart
Ligustrum ovalifolium and other Privet	18 in. apart
Pyracantha coccinea lalandi	24 in. apart
Ribes alpinum - Alpine currant	15 in. apart
Tallhedge Buckthorn	24 in. apart
Taxus, upright varieties	24 in. apart
Thuja occidentalis nigra	24 in. apart
Tsuga canadensis	5 ft. apart
Viburnum opulus nanum	12 in. apart

* may need to be modified for special situations or regions of country

SIZE OF EXCAVATIONS FOR PLANTING

Kind of Plant	Size of Plant	Diameter of Hole (Minimum)	Depth of Hole (Minimum)
	Caliper in Inches	Feet	Inches
Trees	Up to 1¼	2½	18
	1¼ - 1½	3	20
	1½ - 1¾	3½	21
	1¾ - 2	4	21
	2 - 2½	4½	22
	2½ - 3	4½	24
	3 - 3½	5	26
	3½ - 4	5	28
	4 - 4½	6	30
	4½ - 5	6	32
	5 - 5½	7	34
	5½ - 6	7	36
	6 - 7	8	38
	7 - 8	9	38
	8 - 9	10	40
	9 - 10	11	42
Shrubs	Height or Spread in Inches	Inches	Inches
	15 - 24	18	15
	Height in Feet	Inches	Inches
	2 - 3	18	18
	3 - 4	24	18
	4 - 5	28	20
	5 - 6	36	20
	6 - 8	42	22
	8 - 10	48	24
Vines and Other Plants	All Sizes	12	12

PLANTING HOLE SUGGESTIONS

Size of shrub	Diameter and depth of planting holes
1 to 2 ft.	16 in. by 10 in.
2 to 3 ft.	18 in. by 12 in.
3 to 4 ft.	20 in. by 14 in.
4 to 6 ft.	24 in. by 18 in.

Size of trees	Diameter and depth of planting holes
6 to 8 ft.	30 in. by 19 in.
1 to 1 1/2 in. cal.	34 in. by 21 in.
1 1/2 to 2 in. cal.	36 in. by 22 in.
2 to 2 1/2 in. cal.	40 in. by 25 in.
2 1/2 to 3 in. cal.	44 in. by 26 in.
3 to 4 in. cal.	52 in. by 30 in.
4 to 5 in. cal.	56 in. by 32 in.

BOX PLANTING INFORMATION

Box Width	Box Depth	Weight	Plant Hole Width	Plant Hole Depth
16″	20″	195#	3′ Sq.	18″
24″	20″	575#	3½	18″
24″	25″	725#	4″	22″
30″	30″	1500#	4½	27″
36″	36″	2600#	5½	32″
42″	38″	3400#	6½	32″

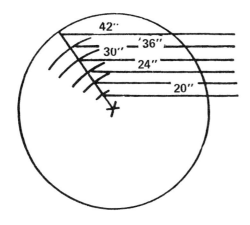

**BOX
DIMENSIONS**

42″ Box
36″ Box
30″ Box
24″ Box
20″ Box

**HOLE
DIAMETER**

5′ 7″ dia
4′11″ dia
4′ 3″ dia
3′ 4″ dia
2′11″ dia

SOME COMMON BROADLEAF WEEDS AND SUGGESTED CHEMICAL CONTROL

Weed	Life Cycle[2]	Recommended Chemical	Time of Application	Degree of Control
Plantain, buckhorn	P	2,4-D or MCPP	fall or spring	good
Plantain, broadleaf	P	2,4-D or MCPP	fall or spring	good
Purslane	A	2,4-D	summer	good
Red sorrel	P	dicamba	spring, summer or fall	good
Speedwell,	P	silvex[1]	spring or fall	fair to good
Spurge, prostrate	A	silvex[1]	spring	fair
Sow thistle	A	2,4-D or dicamba	fall	good
Starwort	P	silvex[1]	fall or spring	fair to good
Thistle	P or B	dicamba or 2,4-D	spring	fair to good
Violet	P	silvex[1] or dicamba	spring	good
White clover	P	silvex[1], MCPP dicamba	spring,	good
Woodsorrel	P	silvex[1]	spring	fair to good
Yarrow	P	silvex[1]	spring	fair

[1] March 1, 1979 the Federal EPA issued emergency suspension of all sales and uses of 2,4,5-TP (Silvex). Any further use of Silvex will be determined by appeals and special expedited hearings of the EPA.

[2] A=Annual, B=Biennial, P=Perrennial, WA=Winter Annual

Weed	Life Cycle[2]	Recommended Chemical	Time of Application	Degree of Control
Black medic	A, B, P	silvex[1] or dicamba	early spring	good
Carrot, wild	B	2,4-D	spring	good
Chickweed, common	WA	silvex[1], MCPP, or dicamba	spring or fall	good
Chickweed, mouse eared	P	silvex[1], MCPP, or dicamba	fall or spring	good
Chickory	P	2,4-D	spring	good
Cinquefoil	P	2,4-D	fall or spring	good
Dandelion	P	2,4-D or MCPP	fall or spring	good
Dock, curly	P	2,4-D or dicamba	fall spring	good
Garlic or onion	P	2,4-D ester	late fall, early spring	fair
Ground Ivy	P	silvex[1] or MCPP	summer, fall	fair to good
Hawkweed	P	2,4-D or dicamba	fall or early spring	good
Heal all	P	2,4-D	spring	good
Henbit	WA or B	silvex[1]	spring	good
Knotweed	A	dicamba	spring to mid-summer	good
Mallow, common	A,B	silvex[1]	spring	fair
Pearlwort	P	MCPP or dicamba	spring or fall	good
Pennywort	P	silvex[1]	summer, fall or spring	good

PLANNING ANNUAL DISPLAY BEDS

There is a simple system to estimate how many plants a bed requires to create an attractive display of annuals.

First determine the number of square feet in the area to be planted. For rectangles, the area is calculated by multiplying length times width. For circles, multiply the radius of the circle squared by 3.1416. Determine the number of square feet in an oval by multiplying 3.1416 times the average radius squared. For triangles, multiply one half the height times the base.

For example, a circle with a radius of 6 feet contains 113.09 square feet (6 feet squared [36] times 3.1416).

The table which follows gives a general guide to the area 100 annual plants can be expected to cover when set out 4 inches apart, 6 inches apart, etc.

100 plants spaced:

4" apart will cover. . . . .   11 square feet
6" apart will cover. . . . .   25 square feet
8" apart will cover. . . . .   44 square feet
10" apart will cover. . . . .   70 square feet
12" apart will cover. . . . . 100 square feet
18" apart will cover. . . . . 225 square feet
24" apart will cover. . . . . 400 square feet

While the above table is a good rule of thumb, it does little more than hint at the growth habits of different annuals; each type of plant requires a varying amount of space for its root system and leaf spread. A mature ageratum might be expected to measure 8" across; a mature impatiens might be 24". Nor does the above table consider the density of display you may wish to create. Naturally, more ageratum would be required to cover 25 square feet densely than would be required if impatiens were selected.

To get an idea of how much space a mature plant will cover, check the desired spacing for the particular plant. Such information is included on seed packages, plant identification tags and general gardening literature. To find the area a mature geranium will cover, multiply the suggested distance between plants (18") by itself. The answer (324 square inches in the case of geraniums) is an approximation of the area one plant will need at maturity.

To apply this information to the area to be planted, compute the square inches of the plot. Do this by multiplying the number of square feet (113.09 for the circle planned earlier) by 144 (the number of square inches per square foot). The answer is the number of square inches in the plot. The circle with a 6-ft. radius contains 16,284.96 square inches.

Divide the number of square inches required for one plant (324 for one geranium) into the number of square inches in the plot (16,284.96 for the circle) and the answer is the number of geraniums to plant in the circular planting bed (50.2).

To find the number of geraniums to use in a circle with a 6-ft. radius:

1. **The number of square feet in a circle = pi (3.1416) x radius^2.**
   Example:
   $3.1416 \times 6^2 = 113.09$ square feet.

2. **The number of square inches in a circle = square feet x inches (144) in a square foot.**
   Example:
   $113.09 \times 144 = 16{,}284.96$ square inches.

3. **The area needed by one plant = recommended spacing^2.**
   Example:
   18" for one geranium $\times$ 18 = 324 square inches for one geranium.

GROUND COVER SPACING

The following table contains a partial but representative list of ground covers and suggested spacing on center. However, there is no hard and fast rule for spacing. Factors as plant sizes available, quality, customers desire for quick cover and budget should be considered. Close planting is desirable for immediate effect, protection of one plant to another and to reduce weed competition. Ground covers, by nature, prefer close company.

	2-1/4 pot or Jiffy 7	1 gal.	B&B	Other
Ajuga	8''	12''	—	—
Arctostaphylos uva-ursi	8''	—	—	—
Cornilla varia 'Penngift'	24''	—	—	—
Euonymus fortunei and varieties	10''	12''	18-24(3 yr)	—
Hedera helix and varieties	8''	12''	—	—
Juniperus horizontalis and varieties	—	18''	—	—
Lonicera japonica	12''	—	—	—
Pachyandra terminalis and varieties	6-8''	—	—	—
Rosa wichuraina	—	—	—	18'' on Center
Vinca minor and varieties	8''	—	—	12''(2yr Clump)
Polygonum alberti	10''	18''	—	—

How to figure the number of ground cover plants required:
Multiply the number of square feet by the number of plants required per square foot using this table:

Distance Apart	Plants Per Sq. Ft.
4''	9.1
6''	4
8''	2.25
9''	1.77
10''	1.44
12''	1
18''	.45
24''	.25
36''	.11

One Flat of 100 Plants Will Cover:

Inch Spacing	Square Feet
4	11
6	25
8	44
10	70
12	100
15	156
18	225
24	400

WATER

RAINFALL: CONVERSION TABLES

Inches of Rainfall	Gallons per Acre	Cubic Feet per Acre	Tons per Acre
1	22,635	3,630	101.1
2	45,270	7,260	202.2
3	67,905	10,890	303.3
4	90,539	14,520	404.4
5	113,174	18,150	505.5
10	226,348	36,300	1,011.0

VOLUME PER UNIT AREA: CONVERSION TABLES

Pints per Square Yard	Gallons per Acre	Inches of Rainfall
1/6	100.0	
1/3	200.0	
1/2	302.5	
2/3	400.0	
1	605.0	
1 1/3	800.0	
1 2/3	1,000.0	
2	1,210.0	
4	2,420.0	
8	4,840.0	
2 1/3	11,300.0	1/2
4 2/3	22,600.0	1
9 1/3	45,200.0	2

UNITS OF WATER MEASUREMENT AND EQUIVALENCES

1 U.S. Gallon	231 Cubic Inches	134 Cubic Feet	8.33 Pounds
1 Cubic Foot	7.48 U.S. Gallons	62.4 Pounds	
1 Acre Foot	43,500 Cubic Feet	325,850 U.S. Gallons	. . 12 Acre Inches
1 Acre Inch	27,154 U.S. Gallons		
1 U.S. Gallon Per Minute . .	.00223 Cubic Feet Per Second		
1 Miner's Inch	11.25 U.S. Gallons Per Minute @ 40 Inches Per Second Feet		
1 Miner's Inch	9.0 U.S. Gallons Per Minute @ 50 Inches Per Second Feet		

1 Cubic Foot Per Second . .		
	7.48	Gallons Per Second
	448.8	Gallons Per Minute
	646,272.0	Gallons Per 24 Hours
	1.983	Acre Feet Per 24 Hours
	40.0	Miner's Inches (In California)

WATER APPLICATION FOR LANDSCAPES

In the irrigation of lawns, whenever possible, no less than 1 inch of water should be put on at each application. Shrubs and trees require even deeper watering to keep root distribution deep and below the turf.

RELATIVE SUSTAINED WATER INTAKE RATES FROM TYPICAL SOILS			
Soil Type	Clean Cultivation	Under Healthy Sod	Under Good Organic Mulch
Light (Coarse sandy loam)	0.8 In/Hr.	1.3 In/Hr.	1.0 — 1.5 In/Hr.
Medium Light (Sandy loam)	0.5 In/Hr.	1.0 In/Hr.	0.8 — 1.3 In/Hr.
Medium Heavy (Silt loam)	0.3 In/Hr.	0.6 In/Hr.	0.4 — 1.0 In/Hr.
Heavy (Silt clay loam)	0.25 In/Hr.	0.5 In/Hr.	0.3 — 0.8 In/Hr.

(These figures are not accurate for any one given soil. These are only an indication of average ratios and differences.)

SLOPE AND ITS EFFECT

Grade Slope	PPT Rate Reduction from Flat as above listed.
0% — 5%	0% — 10%
5% — 10%	10% — 20%
10% — 15%	20% — 45%
15% — 20%	45% — 60%
Over 20%	60% on Up

Water flow is controlled by many factors: the meter size, the size of pipe used, the available water pressure, the size and type of head to be used, are all variable factors which will affect the installation and operation of your sprinkler system.

WATER METER CAPACITY

Meter Size in Inches	Safe Maximum* Working Capacity
5/8"	20 Gal/Min.
3/4"	30 Gal/Min.
1"	50 Gal/Min.
1 1/2"	100 Gal/Min.
2"	160 Gal/Min.
4"	500 Gal/Min.

*When Static Pressure is:	Reduce Maximum as listed above to --% Maximum
40 lb. PSI	50%
50 lb. PSI	60%
75 lb. PSI	65%
100 lb. PSI	75%

STEEL PIPE CAPACITY

Pipe Size	Practical Maximum* Water Flow Expected
1/2"	3 — 4 Gal/Min.
3/4"	6 — 8 Gal/Min.
1"	12 — 15 Gal/Min.
1 1/4"	25 — 30 Gal/Min.
1 1/2"	35 — 45 Gal/Min.
2 1/2"	110 — 130 Gal/Min.
3"	200 — 250 Gal/Min.
4"	400 — 500 Gal/Min.

*These will decrease with pressure drop and increased pipe length.

Note may be made here that in general a jump of one or two pipe sizes over meter size balances meter and pipe flow.

Therefore, considering the above data using a conventional type stationary sprinkler head with a 2.5 gal/min. discharge and a rated 100 sq. ft. coverage, it would require a flow of 25 gal/min. to cover 1,000 sq. ft. when taken off one valve. If you have a water pressure of 40 pounds/sq. in. to get coverage you would need a 1 inch meter and one 1 1/2 inch pipe size from the meter into the valve to provide this. If you only have a 3/4 inch meter and a 1 inch line, it would require two valves each covering only 500 sq. ft. to give adequate water if the same heads are used.

SPRINKLER HEAD
Minimum Specifications

Head shall be designed and adjusted so that it delivers no more than 1.0 inch of water per hour nor less water per hour nor less than 0.25 inches averaged over designed distribution area.

To Insure Maximum 1 inch/hr. Precipitation Rate (62.3 gal/100 sq. ft.)
Check Column (A) Against Column (D)

(A) Designed Spacing or Diameter per Head (in Feet)	(B) Area of Coverage Per Head (Sq. Feet)	(C) Approx. Gal. to Provide 1" Water Per Hour	(D) Maximum Gal. Per Minute Per Head
8	50	31	0.5
12	113	70	1.2
16	201	125	2.1
20	314	195	3.2
24	452	282	4.7
28	616	384	6.4
32	804	500	8.3
36	8,018	634	10.6
40	1,257	783	13.1
60	2,827	1,761	29.3
80	5,026	3,131	52.1
100	7,854	4,893	81.5
120	11,309	7,046	117.4
140	15,394	9,588	159.6
160	20,106	12,528	208.8

Water shall be put down in a relatively uniform distribution pattern, with no more than a 20% variation either way from average measuring in pans set at head and every 36 inches from head out through 80% of its designed distribution pattern.

Water shall be delivered in large enough particles to prevent excessive "mist" and loss of water in a gentle (2—4 MPH) breeze on a warm day. Water drops shall also be small enough to not cause excessive splash erosion on new sandy loam soil.

Head type and size shall be selected to permit proper designing for existing conditions involved such as available water volume, pressure, quality (free from solids), etc., as well as sizes and shapes of areas to be covered.

All heads served from the same valve shall have similar precipitation rates to provide uniform control.

All heads shall be designed and constructed to be relatively safe in use and to be fully functional as described and specified to meet use needs.

UNITS OF WATER MEASUREMENT AND EQUIVALENCIES

1 U.S. Gallon	= 231 Cubic Inches	= 134 Cubic Feet	= 8.33 Pounds
1 Cubic Foot	= 7.48 U.S. Gallons	= 62.4 Pounds	
1 Acre Foot	= 43,560 Cubic Feet	= 325,850 U.S. Gallons	= 12 Acre Inches
1 Acre Inch	= 27,154 U.S. Gallons		
1 U.S. Gallon per Minute	= .00223 Cubic Feet per Second		
1 Miner's Inch	= 11.25 U.S. Gallons per Minute @ 40 Inches per Second Feet		
1 Miner's Inch	= 9.0 U.S. Gallons per Minute @ 50 Inches per Second Feet		

1 Cubic Foot per Second =

7.48	Gals/Second
448.8	Gals/Minute (gpm)
646,272.0	Gals/24 Hours
1.983	Acre Feet/24 Hours
40.0	Miner's Inches (In California)

CAPACITY OF ROUND POOLS PER FOOT OF DEPTH

Diameter	Gallons	Diameter	Gallons
3'0	52.88	15'0	1321.90
3'6''	71.97	16'0	1504.10
4'0	94.00	19'0	2120.90
4'6''	118.97	20'0	2350.10
5'0	155.00	21'0	2591.00
6'0	211.51	22'0	2843.60
7'0	287.88	23'0	3108.00
8'0	376.01	24'0	3384.10
9'0	475.89	25'0	3672.00
10'0	587.52	26'0	3971.60
11'0	710.90	27'0	4283.00
12'0	846.03	28'0	4606.20
13'0	992.91	29'0	4941.00
14'0	1151.50	30'0	5287.70

To find the capacity of pools greater than shown above, find a tank of one-half the size desired, and multiply its capacity by four, or find one one-third the size desired and multiply its capacity by 9.

WATER MEASUREMENT

1 Imperial gal. = 10 lbs. = 0.16 cu. ft. = 4.54 l
1 U.S. gal. = 8.33 lbs. = 0.13 cu. ft. = 3.79 l
1 ton of water = 36 cu. ft.
= 224 gals.
1 ft. head of water = 0.434 lbs. per sq. in. (p.s.i.)
1 lb. per sq. in. (p.s.i.) = 2.3 ft. head of water
= 14.7 lbs. per sq. in. (p.s.i.)
= 30 in. of mercury (inHg)

$$\text{Water horsepower} = \frac{\text{gals. per min.} \times \text{total head in ft.}}{3,300}$$

Horsepower required to drive pumps =

$$\frac{\text{water hp} \times 100}{\text{efficiency percentage of motor or engine}}$$

WATER MEASUREMENT
Flow of Water Through Nozzles
VOLUME OF WATER DELIVERED—BY SIZE OF HOSE

Water Pressure (Lbs.)	Hose Diameter						
	3/8″	13/32″	7/16″	1/2″	9/16″	3/4″	5/8″
30	2.6	3.2	3.8	5.3	7.2	9.3	14.5
40	3.5	4.2	5.0	7.0	9.4	12.2	19.0
50	4.3	5.2	6.3	8.8	11.8	15.3	24.0
60	5.2	6.2	7.5	10.5	14.1	18.3	28.5
70	6.0	7.3	8.7	12.2	16.2	21.0	32.7
80	6.8	8.3	9.9	13.9	18.5	24.0	37.3

Note: Table based on 50-foot hose length: For 25 feet multiply by 1.40; for 75 feet, by 0.80.

WATER

MATERIALS

SOIL COVERAGE IN SQUARE FEET PER CUBIC YARD

Depth in Inches	Coverage in Square Feet
1/8	2,592
1/4	1,296
3/8	864
1/2	648
5/8	518
3/4	432
1	324
2	162
3	108
4	81
5	67
6	54
8	40
10	33
12	27

Example: Area to be covered is 2,160 Square Feet to a depth of 4 Inches.
From the chart, find that 1 Cubic Yard will cover 81 Square Feet to 4 Inches.

$$\frac{2,160}{81} = 26.67 \text{ Cubic Yards required.}$$

APPROXIMATE VOLUMES OF SAND OR GRAVEL IN STOCK FILE
Assuming Angle of Repose 37°
Volume Equals 1/3 B H
B Equals Area of Base

Height H in Feet	Volume Cu. Yds.	Height H in Feet	Volume Cu. Yds.
10	68	60	14,800
15	230	65	18,750
20	550	70	23,400
25	1,080	75	28,800
30	1,640	80	34,600
35	2,900	85	41,800
40	4,350	90	49,700
45	6,200	95	58,300
50	8,500	100	68,350

TOP DRESSINGS–COVERAGES IN CUBIC FEET AND CUBIC YARDS

Depth in Inches	For 1,000 Square Feet in Cubic Feet	in Cubic Yards	For One Acre in Cubic Yards
1/8	10.53	.39	17
1/4	21.0	.78	34
3/8	30.5	1.17	51
1/2	42.0	1.56	68
5/8	52.5	1.95	85
3/4	63.0	2.34	102
1	84.0	3.12	136
2	168.0	6.24	272

Example: 1/2″ coverage is required over 2,000 Square Feet.
From the chart, find that 1/2″ coverage will require **1.56 Cubic Yards per 1,000 Square Feet.**
1.56 × 2 = 3.12 Cubic Yards material.

MATERIALS

NURSERY CONTAINER STOCK
Approximate Back-Fill Volume For Various Container Stock
Square Plant-Pits/Vertical Sides

	Plant Pit Volume in Cubic Feet		Container Stock Displacement in Cubic Feet		Back-Fill Necessary* Cubic Feet	Cubic Yards
(1 gal.)	.7	(minus)	.15	(equals)	.55	0.02
(5 gal.)	3.7	—	.60	=	3.10	0.115
(15 gal.)	12.5	—	2.00	=	10.50	0.40
(16″ Box)	14.2	—	2.50	=	11.70	0.43
(20″ Box)	22.2	—	4.75	=	17.45	0.64
(24″ Box)	32.0	—	6.70	=	25.30	0.94
(30″ Box)	45.5	—	13.60	=	31.90	1.20
(36″ Box)	80.6	—	23.40	=	57.20	2.10
(42″ Box)	112.7	—	31.70	=	81.00	3.00
(48″ Box)	168.7	—	40.30	=	128.40	4.75
(54″ Box)	216.7	—	56.00	=	160.70	5.90
(60″ Box)	283.5	—	74.40	=	209.10	7.74

*Shrinkage Factor not applied. See Table for shrinkage of various soil types.

TREE PIT EXCAVATION FOR NURSERY CONTAINER STOCK
Round Pits/Vertical Sides

Container Size	Pit Diameter in Inches	Pit Depth in Inches	Volume Displacement* in Cubic Feet
1 Gallon	12	12	0.78
5 Gallon	20	20	3.60
15 Gallon	32	24	11.10
16″ Box	34	24	12.60
20″ Box	36	24	14.10
24″ Box	40	24	17.40
30″ Box	50	27	30.60
36″ Box	60	32	52.36
42″ Box	68	32	67.20
48″ Box	80	36	104.70
54″ Box	90	36	132.50
60″ Box	100	42	190.80

*Swellage Factor not applied. See Table for swellage of various soil types.

MATERIALS

WEIGHTS OF MATERIALS

Earth	Pounds per Cubic Foot	Pounds per Cubic Yard	Cubic Yards per Ton	Tons per Cubic Yard
Clay (wet)	105 - 120	2,835 - 3,240	.71 - .62	1.42 - 1.62
Clay (dry)	90 - 110	2,430 - 2,970	.82 - .67	1.22 - 1.49
Granite	170	4,590	.44	2.30
Gravel	120 - 135	3,240 - 3,645	.62 - .55	1.62 - 1.82
Loam (dry—compact)	90 - 100	2,430 - 2,700	.82 - .74	1.22 - 1.35
Loam (dry—loose)	75 - 90	2,025 - 2,430	.99 - .82	1.01 - 1.22
Peat Moss (compact)	15 - 18	405 - 486	4.9 - 4.1	.20 - .24
Peat Moss (loose)	3 - 5	81 - 135	24.7 - 14.8	.04 - .07
Sand (dry)	95 - 110	2,565 - 2,970	.78 - .67	1.28 - 1.49
Sand (wet)	120 - 130	3,240 - 3,510	.62 - .57	1.62 - 1.76
Silt (wet)	130 - 145	3,510 - 3,915	.57 - .51	1.76 - 1.96

COMPUTATION OF VOLUME MATERIALS—TRENCH EXCAVATION
Cubic Yards Per 100 Lineal Feet*

Depth in Inches	Trench Width in Inches						
	12"	18"	24"	30"	36"	42"	48"
6	1.9	2.8	3.7	4.6	5.6	6.6	7.4
12	3.7	5.6	7.4	9.3	11.1	13.0	14.8
18	5.6	8.3	11.1	13.9	16.7	19.4	22.3
24	7.4	11.1	14.8	18.5	22.2	26.0	29.6
30	9.3	13.8	18.5	23.2	27.8	32.4	37.0
36	11.1	16.6	22.2	27.8	33.3	38.9	44.5
42	13.0	19.4	25.9	32.4	38.9	45.4	52.0
48	14.8	22.2	29.6	37.0	44.5	52.0	59.2

*Measured as soil in place.

Example: Trench 30" deep x 18" wide x 100 lineal feet = $\frac{375}{27}$ = 13.8 Cubic Yards.

[On chart, the quantity at the intersection of depth (30) and width (18).]

THE "FEEL" CHART

Degree of Moisture	Feel	Amount of Moisture
Dry	Powder Dry	None
Low	Crumbly, will not hold together	25 percent or less (critical)
Fair	Somewhat crumbly, but will hold together	25 to 50 percent
Good	Forms ball; will stick slightly with pressure	50 to 75 percent
Excellent	Forms a ball and is pliable; sticks readily; a clear water sheen will come to the surface when ball is squeezed in the hand	75 to 100 percent
Too Wet	Can squeeze free water	Over field capacity

WEIGHTS OF MATERIALS

Material	Weight per cubic foot (1b)	Weight per cubic yard (cwt)	Cu feet per ton
Granite	166		
Marble	170		
Portland stone	135–145		
Slate	160–180		
York stone	130–150		
Brickwork (average)	115		
Concrete: lightweight	90		
Concrete: precast	130		
Concrete: reinforced	150		
Lime	53		
Plaster	50		
Timber: hardwood (av.)	45		
Timber: softwood (av.)	35		
Cast iron	450		
Steel	490		
Bronze	513		
Pebbles	110		
Humus: dry	35		
Humus: wet	82		
Subsoil, *in situ*: dry	110		
Subsiol, *in situ*: wet	125		
Mud	100		
Clay soil: compacted, dry	75–100		16–18
Clay soil: compacted, wet	125		
Clay soil: loose dug		26	18–22
Loam: *in situ*: dry	80		23–25
Loam: *in situ*: wet	120		
Loam loose dug	75	23	25–27
Sandy loam: *in situ*			21–23
Sandy loam: loose dug		23	15–17
Dry Sand	95–110	22	23–25
Wet Sand	110–130	30	17–19
Gravel	110	28	16–20
Chalk	125	34	13–15
Limestone	135	40	13–14
Marl		25	19–21
Sandstone	125	37	14–16
Shale	150	38	12–14
Peat: dry		7	60–70
Peat: wet		14	33–36
Shingle	110	36	
Flints		48	

COMPUTATION
VOLUME OF EXCAVATED MATERIAL

(Depth in inches and feet)	(Cubic yards per square surface foot)
2″	.006
4″	.012
6″	.018
8″	.025
10″	.031
1′	.037
2′	.074
3′	.111
4′	.148
5′	.185
6′	.222
7′	.259
8′	.296
9′	.332
10′	.369

*(no swellage factor applied)

Example:
Excavation required: 20′ x 30′ x 4′ = 600 times .148 = 88.8 Cu. Yds.

NURSERY CONTAINER STOCK
VOLUME OF EXCAVATED SOIL RESULTING FROM MULTIPLE PLANTINGS
SQUARE PLANTING PITS

Container Stock	**Excavation Yardage per:		
	10 Plants	100 Plants	1,000 Plants
1 Gallon	0.24	2.40	24.00
5 Gallon	1.37	13.70	137.00
15 Gallon	4.60	46.00	460.00
16″ Box	5.26	52.60	526.00
20″ Box	8.22	82.20	822.00
24″ Box	11.80	118.00	1180.00
30″ Box	17.00	170.00	1700.00
36″ Box	30.00	300.00	3000.00
42″ Box	41.70	417.00	4170.00
48″ Box	62.50	625.00	6250.00
54″ Box	80.00	800.00	8000.00
60″ Box	100.50	1005.00	10050.00

*Swellage factor not applied.

APPROXIMATE SWELLAGE FACTORS
FOR VARIOUS SOIL TYPES
(calculated from 100% volume in place to
excavated and loose material ready for transport.)

SOIL TYPE	90% relative compaction (factor)	excavated and loose (factor)
Sand	1	1.15
Sandy-Loam	1	1.20
Clay-Loam	1	1.30
Clay	1	1.35

(example) 400 cu yds clay-loam compact and in place
will require haulage of 400 x 1.3 cu yds material.
(400 x 1.3 = 520 cu yds)

TOP DRESSINGS:
COVERAGES IN CUBIC FEET AND CUBIC YARDS

Depth In Inches	For 1,000 Sq. Ft. In Cu. Ft.	For 1,000 Sq. Ft. In Cu. Yds.	For one acre In Cu. Yds.
1/8"	10.53	.39	17
1/4"	21.0	.78	34
3/8"	30.5	1.17	51
1/2"	42.0	1.56	68
5/8"	52.5	1.95	85
3/4"	63.0	2.34	102
1"	84.0	3.12	136
2"	168.0	6.24	272

Example: 1/2" coverage is required over 2,000 Sq. Ft.
From the chart: 1/2" coverage will require 1.56 Cu. Yds. per
1,000 Sq. Ft. 1.56 x 2 = 3.12 cubic yards material.

SOILS—ANGLES OF REPOSE

Soil	Degrees from Horizontal		
	Dry	Moist	Wet
Sand	20-35	30-45	20-40
Loam	20-40	25-45	35-55
Gravel	30-50		

"Angle of Repose" is interpreted to mean "the slope which a given material will maintain without sliding."

ANGLE OF REPOSE OF VARIOUS SOILS

Soil	Degrees
Firm earth (in situ)	50
Loose earth or vegetable soil	28
Firm clay	45
Wet clay	16
Dry sand	38
Wet sand	22

SOIL: HAND TEST FOR TEXTURE

Work a handful of MOIST soil in the fingers:

If it is gritty and fails to soil the fingers . . . . **Sand**

If it is gritty but soils the fingers and can be pressed roughly into a ball . . . . **Sandy-loam**

If it is 'sticky,' easily molded in the fingers and quickly 'polished' by sliding between the finger and thumb . . **Clay-loam**

If it is sticky, stiff and plastic enough to be rolled into long flexible 'worms' . . . . **Clay**

If it is not sticky, nor can be polished, but feels 'silky' or 'soapy,' and can be molded but is not cohesive . . . . **Silty-loam**

If it is neither gritty, sticky nor silky . . . . **Medium-loam**

DEFINITIONS

Loam: a mixture of clay, sand and silt in fairly balanced proportions
Marl: a mixture of clay and chalk

WEIGHTS

Sandy Soil, Dry

Cu. ft.   =   90 pounds
Cu. yd. = 2,430 pounds
Bushel =   112 pounds

Pint water   =   1.04 pounds
Gallon water =   8.34 pounds
Gallon water =   3,785 grams

Pound = 7,000 grains
Pound =   453 grams
Pound =   16 ounces (Avoir)

Loamy Soil, Dry

Cu. ft.   =   80 pounds
Cu. yd. = 3,160 pounds
Bushel =   100 pounds

Gram =   15.43 grains
Gram =   0.035 ounces (Avoir)
Gram =   1,000 milligrams

Cu. ft. water = 62.2 pounds

Clayey Soil, Dry

Cu. ft.   =   75 pounds
Cu. yd. = 2,025 pounds
Bushel =   94 pounds

Ounce (Avoir.) = 437.5 grains
Ounce (Avoir.) = 28.35 grams
Ounce (Avoir.) =   0.06 pounds

LUMBER BOARD MEASUREMENTS

To find the number of board feet in a piece of lumber, multiply the length in feet by the width in inches and the thickness in inches and divide by 12.

LUMBER BOARD FOOT TABLE

Timber Size in Inches	Length in Feet						
	8	10	12	14	16	18	20
1 x 2	1.3	1.7	2.0	2.3	2.7	3.0	3.3
1 x 3	2.0	2.5	3.0	3.5	4.0	4.5	5.0
1 x 4	2.7	3.3	4.0	4.7	5.3	6.0	6.6
1 x 6	4.0	5.0	6.0	7.0	8.0	9.0	10.0
1 x 10	6.7	8.3	10.0	11.7	13.3	15.0	16.7
1 x 12	8.0	10.0	12.0	14.0	16.0	18.0	20.0
1 x 14	9.3	11.7	14.0	16.3	18.7	21.0	23.3
2 x 4	5.3	6.7	8.0	9.3	10.7	12.0	13.3
2 x 6	8.0	10.0	12.0	14.0	16.0	18.0	20.0
2 x 8	10.7	13.3	16.0	18.7	21.3	24.0	26.7
2 x 10	13.3	16.7	20.0	23.3	26.7	30.0	33.3
2 x 12	16.0	20.0	24.0	28.0	32.0	36.0	40.0

CONVERSION OF LUMBER SIZES TO FEET BOARD MEASURE

Feet Board Measure of Lumber per Linear Foot for Various Lumber Sizes

Size	F.B.M./Lin. Ft.	Size	F.B.M./Lin. Ft.	Size	F.B.M./Lin. Ft.
1 x 2	0.167	2 x 8	1.334	4 x 10	3.334
1 x 3	0.250	2 x 10	1.667	4 x 12	4.000
1 x 4	0.334	2 x 12	2.000	6 x 6	3.000
1 x 6	0.500	2 x 14	2.334	6 x 8	4.000
1 x 8	0.667	2 x 16	2.667	6 x 10	5.000
1 x 10	0.834	3 x 4	1.000	6 x 12	6.000
1 x 12	1.000	3 x 6	1.500	6 x 14	7.000
1 x 14	1.167	3 x 8	2.000	8 x 8	5.334
1 x 16	1.334	3 x 10	2.500	8 x 10	6.667
1 x 18	1.500	3 x 12	3.000	8 x 12	8.000
1 x 20	1.667	3 x 14	3.500	10 x 10	8.334
2 x 2	0.334	3 x 16	4.000	10 x 12	10.000
2 x 3	0.500	4 x 4	1.334	10 x 14	11.667
2 x 4	0.667	4 x 6	2.000	12 x 12	12.000
2 x 6	1.000	4 x 8	2.667	12 x 16	16.000

142

FEET BOARD MEASURE

Length in Feet

Size	8	10	12	14	16	18	20	22	24
				Feet, Board Measure					
1 by 4	2-2/3	3-1/3	4	4-2/3	5-1/3	6	6-2/3	7-1/3	8
1 by 6	4	5	6	7	8	9	10	11	12
1 by 8	5-1/3	6-2/3	8	9-1/3	10-2/3	12	13-1/3	14-2/3	16
1 by 10	6-2/3	8-1/3	10	11-2/3	13-1/3	15	16-2/3	18-1/3	20
1 by 12	8	10	12	14	16	18	20	22	24
2 by 4	5-1/3	6-2/3	8	9-1/3	10-2/3	12	13-1/3	14-2/3	16
2 by 6	8	10	12	14	16	18	20	22	24
2 by 8	10-2/3	13-1/3	16	18-2/3	21-1/3	24	26-2/3	29-1/3	32
2 by 10	13-1/3	16	20	23-1/3	26-2/3	30	33-1/3	36-2/3	40
2 by 12	16	20	24	28	32	36	40	44	48
2 by 14	18-2/3	23-1/3	28	32-2/3	37-1/3	42	46-2/3	51-1/3	56
2 by 16	21-1/3	26-2/3	32	37-1/3	42-2/3	48	53-1/3	58-2/3	64
3 by 6	12	15	18	21	24	27	30	33	36
3 by 8	16	20	24	28	32	36	40	44	48
3 by 10	20	25	30	35	40	45	50	55	60
3 by 12	24	30	36	42	48	54	60	66	72
3 by 14	28	35	42	49	56	63	70	77	84
3 by 16	32	40	48	56	64	72	80	88	96
4 by 4	10-2/3	13-1/3	16	18-2/3	21-1/3	24	26-2/3	29-1/3	32
4 by 6	16	20	24	28	32	36	40	44	48
4 by 8	21-1/3	26-2/3	32	37-1/3	42-2/3	48	53-1/3	58-2/3	64
4 by 10	26-2/3	33-1/3	40	46-2/3	53-1/3	60	66-2/3	73-1/3	80
4 by 12	32	40	48	56	64	72	80	88	96
4 by 14	37-1/3	46-2/3	56	65-1/3	74-2/3	84	93-1/3	102-2/3	112
4 by 16	42-2/3	53-1/3	64	74-2/3	85-1/3	96	106-2/3	117-1/3	128
6 by 6	24	30	36	42	48	54	60	66	72
6 by 8	32	40	48	56	64	72	80	88	96
6 by 10	40	50	60	70	80	90	100	110	120
6 by 12	48	60	72	84	96	108	120	132	144
6 by 14	56	70	84	96	112	126	140	154	166
6 by 16	64	80	96	112	128	144	160	176	192
8 by 8	42-2/3	53-1/3	64	74-2/3	85-1/3	96	106-2/3	117-1/3	128
8 by 10	53-1/3	66-2/3	80	93-1/3	106-2/3	120	133-1/3	146-2/3	160
8 by 12	64	80	96	112	128	144	160	176	192
8 by 14	74-2/3	93-1/3	112	130-2/3	149-1/3	168	186-2/3	205-1/3	224
8 by 16	85-1/3	106-2/3	128	149-1/3	170-2/3	192	213-1/3	234-2/3	256
10 by 10	66-2/3	83-1/3	100	116-2/3	133-1/3	150	166-2/3	183-1/3	200
10 by 12	80	100	120	140	160	180	200	220	240
10 by 14	93-1/3	116-2/3	140	163-1/3	186-2/3	210	233-1/3	256-2/3	280
10 by 16	106-2/3	133-1/3	160	186-2/3	213-1/3	240	266-2/3	293-1/3	320

MATERIALS

APPROXIMATE BOARD FOOT CONTENT
OF SAWED RAILROAD TIES

Grade	End Dimension in Inches	Length in Feet Narrow Gauge: 6.5′	Standard Gauges: 8.0′	8.5′
1	6″ x 6″	20	24	26
2	6″ x 7″	23	28	30
3	6″ x 8″	26	32	34
3	7″ x 7″	27	33	35
4	7″ x 8″	30	37	40
5	7″ x 9″	—	42	45

*Weights per Tie: Extremely variable due to differences in age and water
contents.
Ranges: Approx. 75 Lbs. to 160 Lbs.

EQUIPMENT

EQUIPMENT AMORTIZATION TABLE

Costs to justify purchases shown in cents per hour. These costs to be added to employee's wage rates.

Purchase Price	1 Year	2 Years	3 Years	4 Years	5 Years	6 Years
10.00	.50	.25	.1667	.1250	.1000	.08333
20.00	1.00	.50	.3333	.2500	.2000	.1667
30.00	1.50	.75	.5000	.3750	.3000	.2500
40.00	2.00	1.00	.6667	.5000	.4000	.3333
50.00	2.50	1.25	.8333	.6250	.5000	.4167
60.00	3.00	1.50	1.000	.7500	.6000	.5000
70.00	3.50	1.75	1.167	.8750	.7000	.5833
80.00	4.00	2.00	1.333	1.000	.8000	.6667
90.00	4.50	2.25	1.500	1.125	.9000	.7500
100.00	5.00	2.50	1.667	1.250	1.000	.8333
200.00	10.00	5.00	3.333	2.500	2.000	1.667
300.00	15.00	7.50	5.000	3.750	3.000	2.500
400.00	20.00	10.00	6.667	5.000	4.000	3.333
500.00	25.00	12.50	8.333	6.250	5.000	4.167
750.00	37.50	18.75	12.50	9.375	7.500	6.250
1,000.00	50.00	25.00	16.67	12.50	10.00	8.333
5,000.00	250.00	125.00	83.33	62.50	50.00	41.67

EXAMPLE: If you buy a $60 tool for your employee to use that will last two years, you should add 1.5 cents per hour to the man's wages to pay for it. Of course, to this you also add repair and fuel costs, etc. This gives you a figure to use when evaluating increased productivity potentials.

EQUIPMENT JUSTIFICATION TABLE

Annual Salary	6,000.00	6,500.00	7,000.00	7,500.00	8,000.00	8,500.00	9,000.00	9,500.00
Hourly Equivalent	3.00	3.25	3.50	3.75	4.00	4.25	4.50	4.75
Cents per Minute	5.00	5.42	5.83	6.25	6.67	7.08	7.50	7.92

EQUIPMENT JUSTIFICATION

To see how many extra dollars worth of equipment you need for one year, find the pay scale column that applies to your labor cost for one man. Follow this column down to your hours per year of improvement needed totaled from Table 2. By referring leftward on this table to "Dollars Justified for Equipment Expenditure," you can plot your individual equipment needs.

	Your Pay Scale for One Man							
Annual Salary	$6,000.00	$7,500.00	$9,000.00	$10,500.00	$12,000.00	$13,500.00	$15,000.00	$16,500.00
Weekly Salary (dollars)	115.00	144.00	174.00	204.00	231.00	261.00	288.00	318.00
Hourly Equiv. (dollars)	3.00	3.75	4.50	5.75	6.00	6.75	7.50	8.25
Cents per Minute	4.98	6.24	7.50	8.73	9.99	11.25	12.48	13.77
Dollars Justified for Equipment Expenditures**	Hours Per Year of Improvement Needed*							
$ 300	21	17	12	12	12	8	8	8
600	37	29	25	21	21	17	17	12
900	54	42	33	29	29	25	21	21
1,200	71	54	46	42	37	33	29	25
1,500	87	71	58	50	46	37	37	33
2,100	121	96	79	71	62	54	50	46
3,000	171	137	112	96	87	75	71	62
6,000	337	270	225	191	171	150	137	125
15,000	836	670	557	478	420	370	337	304

*These figures based on 250 eight-hour days per year or 2,000 working hours per year.
**These figures based on replacement after an average life expectancy of six years per unit of equipment.

MOWING POTENTIALS*
COMMERCIAL REEL-TYPE

Sq. Ft. Lawn	18″ Hand	18″ Power Sp	25″ Power Walk	25″ Ride	58″ Ride
1,000	10 min.	5 min.	3 min.	2 min.	
2,000	20 min.	10 min.	6 min.	4 min.	
3,000	30 min.	15 min.	9 min.	6 min.	
4,000	40 min.	20 min.	12 min.	8 min.	
5,000	55 min.	25 min.	15 min.	10 min.	5 min.
6,000	1 hr. 20 min.	35 min.	18 min.	12 min.	6 min.
7,000	1 hr. 40 min.	45 min.	21 min.	14 min.	7 min.
8,000	2 hrs.	55 min.	24 min.	16 min.	8 min.
9,000	2 hrs. 25 min.	65 min.	27 min.	18 min.	9 min.
10,000		1 hr. 25 min.	32 min.	20 min.	10 min.
20,000		3 hrs.	1 hr. 10 min.	45 min.	20 min.
30,000		5 hrs.	1 hr. 45 min.	1 hr. 10 min.	30 min.
1 acre			2 hrs. 20 min.	1 hr. 30 min.	40 min.
2 acres			5 hrs.	3 hrs.	1 hr. 20 min.
5 acres				7 hrs.	3 hrs. 20 min.

*This table assumes that after you get over 30 to 40 minutes of mowing time on an industrial area, you are reaching a critical point—time and cost wise. This is especially true if your area is being used exclusively for mood and setting purposes.

LAWN MOWERS

Reel Type—Must be a quality, well established "name brand" machine with adequate service and repair center readily available.

Mower must have adjustable mowing height adaptation. For cool season grass areas (Kentucky Bluegrass, etc.) adjustments must include 1½" to 2½". For warm season grass areas (Bermuda, Zoisia Grasses, etc.) ½" to 1½". These adjustments must be made easily, requiring no unusual tools and accomplished without tipping engine or bed knife out of proper position.

Must have positive hold action clutch system that cannot slip in or out of gear during operation or idling.

Power mowers shall be equipped with three-section rollers or better, all power mowers shall be self-propelled.

MOWER RELATIONSHIPS

Mower Size	Max. Weight	Min. H.P.	Number of Blades for Cut Type	
			High	Low
16" Hand	40 lbs.	Hand	5	5
16" - 19" Power	95 lbs.	2	5	6
20" - 21" Power	110 lbs.	2¼	5	6
22" - 25" Power	145 lbs.	3	5	6

All powered units shall have four-cycle engines of a quality name.

All mowers shall be of a sturdy, commercial-type construction.

Some companies making machines that meet these specifications are:

Power Mower	**Hand Mower**
Hahn - Eclipse	Pennsylvania
Cooper	Great States
Toro	Sears
National	
Jacobson (4-Cycle)	

Size and Cost determined on lawn area involved.

POWER MOWING—ACRES PER HOUR
APPROXIMATE PERFORMANCE—POWERED OR TRACTOR DRAWN MOWERS
(BASED ON MOWER EFFECTIVE CUTTING WIDTHS AND VARYING SPEEDS IN MILES PER HOUR)
SMALLER UNITS—NOT COMPUTED BEYOND 5 MPH

MPH	Width in Inches										
	18	20	25	30	36	42	60	70	76	84	86
1.5	.23	.24	.30	.36	.44	.53	.72	.79	.91	1.02	1.03
2.0	.30	.32	.40	.48	.58	.72	.96	1.12	1.22	1.40	1.50
3.0	.45	.48	.60	.72	.87	1.02	1.45	1.68	1.83	2.04	2.07
4.0	.60	.64	.80	.96	1.16	1.36	1.92	2.24	2.44	2.72	2.76
5.0	.75	.80	1.00	1.20	1.45	1.70	2.43	2.80	3.05	3.40	3.45

Figures at 80% maximum efficiency.

REEL MOWERS—FAIRWAYS—TRACTOR DRAWN
TYPICAL COMBINATIONS

Units in Gang	Cutting Width	Height of Cut
3	6' - 10.0''	½'' to 3¼''
5	11' - 2.9''	½'' to 3¼''
7	15' - 5.9''	½'' to 3¼''
9	19' - 10.5''	½'' to 3¼''
11	24' - 1.0''	½'' to 3¼''
13	28' - 6.0''	½'' to 3¼''

152

TYPICAL REEL MOWERS–SELF PROPELLED
SINGLE UNIT GREENS MOWERS

Model	Cutting Width	Height of Cut Range	No. Blades	Speed (MPH)
Greenmaster[†]	21″	1/8″ to 11/16″	9	4.60
Greens Mower*	22″	3/16″ to 1 1/8″	9	3.88

[†]Courtesy Toro Manufacturing Company
*Courtesy Jacobsen Manufacturing Company

TYPICAL REEL MOWERS–SELF PROPELLED
SINGLE UNIT WALKING

Model	Cutting Width	Rated HP	Blades	Approx. Weight
Snapper: C-19-3	19″	3	5	140 lbs.
Snapper: C-21-3	21″	3	5 or 7	155 lbs.
Snapper: C-21-5	21″	5	5 or 7	170 lbs.
Snapper: C-25-5	25″	5	5 or 7	191 lbs.
Snapper: C-27-5	27″	5	5 or 7	197 lbs.
Snapper: C-30-5	30″	5	5 or 7	295 lbs.

Courtesy McDonough-Starlite, Inc.

EQUIPMENT

TYPICAL REEL MOWERS—SELF PROPELLED
RIDING/MULTIPLE UNITS

Model	Cutting Width	Height of Cut Range	HP	Reels	Blades	Speed	Work Cap.
Professional 70[†]	70"	1/2" to 2 1/2"	6.25	3	5 or 6	3 mph	14A/Day
Professional 76[†]	76"	3/8" to 2 1/2"	9.2	3	5 or 6	4.5 mph	26A/Day
Turf King 84*	84"	3/8" to 2 3/4"	12.0	3	5	4.0 mph	22A/Day
F-133*	133"	5/8" to 2"	18.0	5	6	7.0 mph	50A/Day

[†]Courtesy Toro Manufacturing Company
*Courtesy Jacobsen Manufacturing Company

TYPICAL REEL MOWERS—TRACTOR MOUNTED
RAM LIFT OR THREE POINT

Model	Cutting Width	Height of Cut Range	Approx. Work Capacity
Jacobsen 3 Gang*	82"	7/8" to 3 1/2"	24 - 28 Acres/Day
Jacobsen 3 Gang*	84"	7/8" to 3 1/2"	24 - 28 Acres/Day
Jacobsen 5 Gang*	130"	7/8" to 3 1/2"	40 - 50 Acres/Day
Park Challenger (3)[†]	84"	1/2" to 4"	24 - 28 Acres/Day
Park Challenger (5)[†]	134"	1/2" to 4"	40 - 50 Acres/Day

*Courtesy Jacobsen Manufacturing Company
[†]Courtesy Roseman Mower Corporation

POWER MOWING—ACRES PER HOUR
APPROXIMATE PERFORMANCE—SELF PROPELLED OR TRACTOR DRAWN

MPH	Widths in Inches							
	134	138	142	168	186	198	246	310
4	4.32	4.48	4.60	5.44	6.00	6.40	7.92	10.00
5	5.40	5.60	5.75	6.80	7.50	8.00	9.90	12.50
6	6.48	6.72	6.90	8.16	9.00	9.60	11.88	15.00
7	7.56	7.84	8.05	9.52	10.50	11.20	13.86	17.50
8	8.64	8.96	9.20	10.88	12.00	12.80	15.84	20.00
9	9.72	10.08	10.35	12.24	13.50	14.40	17.82	22.50
10	10.80	11.20	11.50	13.60	15.00	16.00	19.80	25.00

Figures at 80% maximum efficiency.

POWER MOWING—MINUTES PER ACRE
APPROXIMATE PERFORMANCE—SELF PROPELLED OR TRACTOR DRAWN

MPH	Mowing Widths in Inches							
	134	138	142	168	186	198	246	310
4	13.80	13.40	13.00	11.00	10.00	9.40	7.50	6.00
5	11.10	10.80	10.40	8.80	8.40	7.50	6.00	4.80
6	9.26	8.98	8.70	7.50	6.60	6.20	5.00	4.00
7	8.00	7.75	7.50	6.30	5.70	5.30	4.30	3.40
8	6.96	6.73	6.50	5.50	5.00	4.60	3.80	3.00
9	6.10	6.00	5.80	4.90	4.40	4.20	3.30	2.60
10	5.50	5.35	5.20	4.40	4.00	3.70	3.00	2.40

Figures at 80% maximum efficiency.

TYPICAL FLAIL (VERTICAL) MOWERS—SELF-PROPELLED

Model	Cutting Width	Height of Cut Range	Remarks
R9	24″	¾″ to 3″	handle control or optionable sulky
B32	32′	¾″ to 3″	handle control or optionable sulky

Courtesy Mott Corporation

AVERAGE PAY LOADS—PICK UP TRUCKS

Size	Average Pay Loads in Lbs.
½ Ton	1,683
¾ Ton	3,446
1 Ton	4,524

TYPICAL FLAIL (VERTICAL) MOWERS—TRACTOR DRAWN

Model	Cutting Width	Height of Cut Range	Remarks
60	60″	¾″ to 3″	three point hitch
72	72″	¾″ to 3″	three point hitch
74	74″	¾″ to 6″	three point hitch
88	87″	¾″ to 6″	three point hitch
HS	48″	¾″ to 6″	self-powered, trailing as tandem units with indicated models
60 + 2 HS	144″	¾″ to 3″	
72 + 2 HS	156″	¾″ to 3″	
74 + 2 HS	158″	¾″ to 6″	
88 + 2 HS	171″	¾″ to 6″	

Courtesy Mott Corporation

TYPICAL ROTARY MOWERS—TRACTOR DRAWN
(Three-Point or Pull)

Model	Cutting Width	Height of Cut Range	Approx. Weight Lbs.
901*	60″	2″ to 10″ above ground	610
906*	84″	2″ to 11″ above ground	1,073
902*	100″	2″ to 11″ above ground	1,344
Flex XV†	180″	¾″ to 15″ above ground	3,354

*Courtesy Ford Motor Company
†Courtesy Servis Equipment Company

MACHINE EXCAVATION–TRENCHING MACHINE AND DRAGLINE
MANHOURS PER HUNDRED (100) CUBIC YARDS

Soil	Item	Manhours			
		Oper. Engr.	Oiler	Laborer	Total
Light	**Dragline:** 2 cubic yard bucket 1 cubic yard bucket ½ cubic yard bucket	0.7 1.1 2.0	0.7 1.1 2.0	0.7 1.1 2.0	2.1 3.3 6.0
Medium	2 cubic yard bucket 1 cubic yard bucket ½ cubic yard bucket	1.3 2.0 3.7	1.3 2.0 3.7	1.3 2.0 3.7	3.9 6.0 11.1
Heavy	2 cubic yard bucket 1 cubic yard bucket ½ cubic yard bucket	1.7 2.7 4.9	1.7 2.7 4.9	1.7 2.7 4.9	5.1 8.1 14.7
Medium	**Trenching Machine:**	3.8		7.5	11.3
Heavy	**Trenching Machine:**	4.8		9.4	14.2

Manhours include operations of excavating and dumping on side lines or loading into trucks for dragline excavation.

Manhours for trenching machine include regular trenching up to 3'6" wide.

Manhours do not include hauling.

Above manhours are based on excavating up to six (6) feet deep. If excavations are to be greater in depth than this, the estimator should consider additional methods, planning, and equipment required.

If total excavated quantity is less than one hundred (100) cubic yards, increase above manhours by thirty (30) percent.

REPRESENTATIVE TILLING EQUIPMENT—TRACTOR DRAWN
WORK RATED CAPACITY MEASURED IN ACRES PER HOUR—VARIOUS SPEEDS

Tillage Swath in Inches	Acres Tilled at Indicated Miles per Hour				
	1 Mph	2 Mph	3 Mph	4 Mph	5 Mph
40	.41	.81	1.21	1.61	2.01
50	.50	1.01	1.51	2.02	2.52
60	.61	1.20	1.82	2.42	3.03
70	.71	1.41	2.12	2.83	3.53
80	.81	1.62	2.42	3.23	4.04
100	1.00	2.02	3.02	4.04	5.04
130	1.32	2.61	3.94	5.25	6.56
160	1.61	3.22	4.84	6.46	8.07
180	1.81	3.64	5.44	7.27	9.08

Courtesy Howard Rotavator Company

TYPICAL SELF PROPELLED SOD CUTTERS

Model	Depth of Cut	Width of Cut	Rated Performance—Sq. Yds./Hr.
HD (with sulky)	2"	24"	1,875
JR4-18	2"	18"	1,150
JR3	2"	12"	660

Courtesy Ryan Equipment Company

VEHICULAR GASOLINE CONSUMPTION
COMPUTATION OF MILES PER GALLON

Miles Driven	5	6	7	8	9	Gallons Used 10	12	14	16	18	20	22
100	20	16.7	14.3	12.5	11.1	10	8.3	7.1	6.2	5.5	5.0	
110	22	18.3	15.7	13.8	12.2	11	9.1	7.8	6.8	6.1	5.5	
120	24	20.0	17.1	15.0	13.3	12	10.0	8.5	7.5	6.6	6.0	5.4
130	26	21.7	18.6	16.3	14.4	13	10.7	9.3	8.1	7.2	6.5	5.9
140	28	23.3	20.0	17.5	15.6	14	11.7	10.0	8.7	7.7	7.0	6.3
150	30	25.0	21.4	18.7	16.6	15	12.5	10.7	9.3	8.3	7.5	6.8
160	32	26.6	22.9	20.0	17.7	16	13.3	11.4	10.0	8.8	8.0	7.2
170	34	28.3	24.3	21.3	18.9	17	14.1	12.1	10.6	9.5	8.5	7.7
180	36	30.0	25.7	22.5	20.0	18	15.0	12.8	11.2	10.0	9.0	8.1
190	38	31.7	27.0	23.8	21.1	19	15.8	13.5	11.8	10.5	9.5	8.6
200	40	33.3	28.6	25.0	22.2	20	16.6	14.4	12.5	11.1	10.0	9.0
210		35.0	30.0	26.2	23.3	21	17.5	15.0	13.1	11.5	10.5	9.5
220		36.7	31.4	27.5	24.4	22	18.3	15.7	13.7	12.2	11.0	10.0
230		38.3	32.9	28.8	25.5	23	19.1	16.4	14.3	12.7	11.5	10.4
240			34.3	30.0	26.6	24	20.0	17.0	15.0	13.3	12.0	10.9
250			35.7	31.2	27.8	25	20.8	17.3	15.6	13.0	12.5	11.3
260			37.0	32.5	28.9	26	21.6	18.5	16.2	14.4	13.0	11.8
270			38.6	33.8	30.0	27	22.5	19.2	16.8	15.0	13.5	12.4
280				35.0	31.1	28	23.3	20.0	17.5	15.5	14.0	12.7
290				36.2	32.2	29	24.1	20.7	18.1	16.0	14.5	13.1
300				37.5	33.3	30	25.0	21.4	18.7	16.6	15.0	13.6
310				38.7	34.4	31	25.8	22.1	19.5	17.2	15.5	14.0
320					35.5	32	26.6	22.8	20.0	17.7	16.0	14.5
330					36.6	33	27.5	23.6	20.6	18.3	16.5	15.0
340					37.8	34	28.3	24.3	21.2	18.8	17.0	15.4
350					38.9	35	29.1	25.0	21.9	19.4	17.5	16.0
360						36	30.0	25.7	22.5	20.0	18.0	16.4
370						37	30.8	26.4	23.1	20.5	18.5	16.9
380						38	31.7	27.1	23.7	21.1	19.0	17.3
390						39	32.5	27.8	24.3	21.6	29.5	17.8
400						40	33.3	28.5	25.0	22.2	20.0	18.2

Miles per Gallon is shown where Miles Driven column and Gallons Used column intersect.
Example: Miles Driven = 270; Gallons Used = 18; Miles per Gallon = 15

MACHINE EXCAVATION–BACK HOE
MANHOURS PER HUNDRED (100) CUBIC YARDS

Soil	Bucket Size	Manhours			
		Oper. Engr.	Oiler	Laborer	Total
Light	1 cubic yard bucket	1.4	1.4	1.4	4.2
	¾ cubic yard bucket	1.5	1.5	1.5	4.5
	½ cubic yard bucket	2.0	2.0	2.0	6.0
Medium	1 cubic yard bucket	2.6	2.6	2.6	7.8
	¾ cubic yard bucket	3.8	3.8	3.8	11.4
	½ cubic yard bucket	4.4	4.4	4.4	13.2
Heavy	1 cubic yard bucket	3.5	3.5	3.5	10.5
	¾ cubic yard bucket	4.0	4.0	4.0	12.0
	½ cubic yard bucket	4.9	4.9	4.9	14.7
Hard Pan	1 cubic yard bucket	4.4	4.4	4.4	13.2
	¾ cubic yard bucket	4.6	4.6	4.6	13.8
	½ cubic yard bucket	6.1	6.1	6.1	18.3
Rock	1 cubic yard bucket	4.4	4.4	4.4	13.2
	¾ cubic yard bucket	4.6	4.6	4.6	13.8
	½ cubic yard bucket	6.1	6.1	6.1	18.3

Manhours include operations of excavating and dumping on side lines or loading into trucks.

Manhours do not include hauling or blasting.

Above manhours are based on excavations up to six (6) feet in depth. If excavations are to be greater in depth than this, the estimator should consider methods, planning and equipment required.

If total excavation quantity is less than one hundred (100) cubic yards, increase above units by thirty (30) percent.

DESIGNS AND HOW TO FIGURE AREA

All through the art of Landscaping, different designs are met with. It is important that the Estimator should know how to figure the area of any design that comes before him, in order to arrive at his quantities.

In this section are given a number of designs, some of which are met with frequently in the plans, while other are met with only occasionally. However, they are all included here from the simple square to more intricate designs for the purpose of reference whenever the occasion arises.

These designs are not drawn to any particular scale, the measurements being given arbitrarily merely to show the method of figuring.

If the office is not supplied with a planimeter for measuring areas, these designs will be a good guide for the Estimator and enable him to arrive at accurate figures for such items as Excavation, Top Soil, Fertilizers, etc. that are called for in the specifications.

Planimeters may be purchased from any firm selling drafting equipment and supplies. Usually any blue printing business will also stock this type of item or can order it. Check your telephone yellow pages for "Draftsmens' Supplies". The cost will vary from $60 to $150. The less expensive models are adequate for most landscape nurserymen and contractors.

UNITS
OF
MEASUREMENT

Unit	Equals
60 Seconds	1 Minute
60 Minutes	1 Hour
24 Hours	1 Day
7 Days	1 Week
52 Weeks	1 Year
365 Days	1 Normal Year
366 Days	1 Leap Year
360 Days	1 Commercial Year
10 Years	1 Decade
100 Years	1 Century

ANGULAR AND CIRCULAR MEASURE

Unit	Equals
60 Seconds	1 Minute
60 Minutes	1 Degree
90 Degrees	1 Right Angle
180 Degrees	1 Straight Angle
360 Degrees	1 Full Circle

UNITS OF LIQUID MEASURE

1 Gill	.5 Cup
1 Gill	7.23 Cubic Inches
2 Gills	1 Cup
2 Gills	14.45 Cubic Inches
2 Cups	1 Pint
4 Gills	1 Pint
1 Pint	28.875 Cubic Inches
2 Pints	1 Quart
4 Quarts	1 Gallon
1 Gallon	8 Pints
1 Gallon	231 Cubic Inches
1 Gallon	32 Gills

UNITS OF CUBIC MEASURE

Unit	Equals
1,000 Cubic Millimeters	1 Cubic Centimeter
1,000 Cubic Centimeters	1 Cubic Decimeter
1,000 Cubic Decimeters	1 Cubic Meter

UNITS OF WEIGHT

Unit	Equals
10 Milligrams	1 Centigram
10 Centigrams	1 Decigram
10 Decigrams	1 Gram
10 Grams	1 Dekagram
10 Dekagrams	1 Hectogram
10 Hectograms	1 Kilogram
1,000 Kilograms	1 Metric Ton

UNITS OF DRY MEASURE

1 Pint	0.5 Quarts
1 Pint	33.6 Cubic Inches
2 Pints	1 Quart
2 Pints	67.2 Cubic Inches
8 Quarts	1 Peck
8 Quarts	537.6 Cubic Inches
4 Pecks	1 Bushel
1 Bushel	32 Quarts
1 Bushel	64 Pints
1 Bushel	2,150.4 Cubic Inches

SQUARE TRACTS OF LAND

(IN SQUARE FEET AND IN ACRES)

*Length Each Side in Feet	Area: Sq. Ft.	Area in Acres	
66.0	4356	0.100	(1/10)
73.8	5445	0.125	(1/8)
85.2	7260	0.166	(1/6)
104.4	10890	0.250	(1/4)
120.5	14520	0.333	(1/3)
147.6	21780	0.500	(1/2)
180.8	32670	0.750	(3/4)
208.7	43560	1.000	1
255.6	65340	1.500	(1 1/2)
295.2	87120	2.000	2
330.0	108900	2.500	(2 1/2)
365.1	130680	3.000	3
466.7	217800	5.000	5

*All Sides Equal in Length.

100' LINEAR MEASUREMENTS $\dfrac{100}{x} + 1$	
Spacing	Plants Needed
12"	101
15"	81
18"	68
21"	58
24"	51
27"	45
30"	41
33"	37
36"	34
39"	32
42"	30
45"	28
48"	26

UNITS OF AREA

100 Sq. Millimeters.	1 Sq. Centimeter
10,000 Sq. Centimeters.	1 Sq. Meter
100 Sq. Meters	1 Are
100 Ares	1 Hectare
100 Hectares	1 Sq. Kilometer

UNITS OF LENGTH

10 Millimeters.	1 Centimeter
10 Centimeters	1 Decimeter
10 Decimeters.	1 Meter
10 Meters	1 Dekameter
10 Dekameters	1 Hectometer
10 Hectometers.	1 Kilometer

UNITS OF LIQUID MEASURE

Unit	Equals
10 Milliliters	1 Centiliter
10 Centiliters	1 Deciliter
10 Deciliters	1 Liter
10 Liters	1 Decaliter
10 Decaliters	1 Hectoliter
10 Hectoliters	1 Kiloliter

UNITS OF VOLUME

1,728 Cubic Inches	1 Cubic Foot
46,656 Cubic Inches	1 Cubic Yard
27 Cubic Feet	1 Cubic Yard

UNITS OF MEASUREMENT

UNITS OF WEIGHT

7,000.0 Grains	1 Pound
437.5 Grains	1 Ounce
16.0 Ounces	1 Pound
100.0 Pounds	1 Hundredweight
20.0 Hundredweight	1 Ton
2,000.0 Pounds	1 Ton

UNITS OF AREA

144 Square Inches	1 Square Foot
1,296 Square Inches	1 Square Yard
9 Square Feet	1 Square Yard
43,560 Square Feet	1 Acre
30.25 Square Yards	1 Square Rod
4,840 Square Yards	1 Acre
160 Square Rods	1 Acre
640 Acres	1 Square Mile

UNITS OF LENGTH

12 Inches	1 Foot
3 Feet	1 Yard
16.5 Feet	1 Rod
5.5 Yards	1 Rod
4 Rods	1 Chain
80 Chains	1 Statute Mile
320 Rods	1 Statute Mile
1,760 Yards	1 Statute Mile
5,280 Feet	1 Statute Mile

UNITS OF MEASUREMENT

MATERIALS MEASUREMENTS

SQUARE MEASURE

144 square inches . . .1 square foot
9 square feet . . . . .2 square yard
30 1/4 square yards . . . .1 square rod
272 1/4 square feet . . . . .1 square rod
160 square rods. . . . .1 acre
640 acres. . . . . .1 square mile

CUBIC MEASURE

1728 cubic inches . . . . .1 cubic foot
27 cubic feet. . . . . . .1 cubic yard
128 cubic feet. . . . . . .1 cord (wood)
321 cubic inches . . . . .1 gallon
2150.4 cubic inches . . . . .1 bushel
40 cubic feet. . . . . . .1 ton (shipping)
1 cubic foot. . . . . .about 4/5 of a bushel

LONG MEASURE

12 inches. . . . . . . .1 foot
3 feet. . . . . .1 yard
16 1/2 feet. . . . . .1 rod

DRY MEASURE

2 pints dry. . . . . . . .1 quart dry
8 quarts dry. . . . . .1 peck
105 quarts dry
7058 cubic inches . . . . .1 standard barrel

LIQUID MEASURE

1 pint . . . . 16 ounces
1 quart . . . . 32 ounces
1 gallon. . . . . .128 ounces
32 1/2 gallons . . . . 1 barrel

MEASURES
Soil, etc.

9 shovels . . . . .1 cu. ft.
1 wheelbarrow. . . . . .3 cu. ft.
9 wheelbarrows . . . . .1 cu. yd.

Granite—Decomposed

1 1/2 ton . . . . .1 cu. yd.

CUBIC OR VOLUME MEASURE:

Cu. ft.	= 1,728 cu. in.		Bushel	= 2150.4 cu. in.
Cu. ft.	= 0.037 cu. yds.		Bushel	= 1.24 cu. ft.
Cu. ft.	= 7.48 gallons		Bushel	= approx. 1/20 cu. yd.
Cu. ft.	= 59.84 pints (liq.)		Bushel	= 35.24 liters
Cu. ft.	= 29.92 quarts (liq.)			
Cu. ft.	= 25.71 quarts (dry)		Liter	= 1,000 cu. cm.
Cu. ft.	= 0.804 bushels		Liter	= 0.035 cu. ft.
Cu. ft.	= 28.32 liters		Liter	= 61.02 cu. in.
Cu. yd.	= 27 cu. ft.			
Cu. yd.	= 46,656 cu. in.		Gallon	= 269 cu. in. (dry)
Cu. yd.	= 202 gallons		Gallon	= 3785 cu. cm.
Cu. yd.	= 1,616 pints (liq.)		Gallon	= 0.134 cu. ft.
Cu. yd.	= 808 quarts (liq.)		Gallon	= 231 cu. in. (liq.)
Cu. yd.	= 21.71 bushels		Peck	= 537.6 cu. in.
Ounce (liq.)	= 1.805 cu. in.		Quart (dry)	= 67.2 cu. in.
Pint (liq.)	= 28.87 cu. in.		Quart (liq.)	= 57.7 cu. in.
Lb. water	= 27.68 cu. in.		Lb. water	= 0.016 cu. ft.

CAPACITY MEASURE, LIQUID:

Fluid ounce	= 2 tablespoons		Teaspoon	= 5 milliliters
Fluid ounce	= 6 teaspoons		Teaspoon	= 0.17 fluid ounces
Fluid ounce	= 29.57 milliliters		Teaspoon	= 60 drops
Fluid ounce	= 1.805 cu. in.		Pint	= 2 cups
Cup	= 8 fluid ounces		Pint	= 16 fluid ounces
Cup	= 0.5 pint		Pint	= 473 milliliters
Cup	= 236.5 milliliters		Pint	= 28.87 cu. in.
Cup	= 0.25 quart		Pint	= 0.125 gallon
Cup	= 16 tablespoons		Pint	= 0.473 liter
Cup	= 48 teaspoons		Pint	= 32 tablespoons
Tablespoon	= 3 teaspoons		Cu. ft.	= 29.22 liq. qt.
Tablespoon	= 15 milliliters		Gallon	= 128 fluid ounces
Tablespoon	= 0.5 fluid ounce		Gallon	= 231 cu. in.
Quart	= 32 fluid ounces		Gallon	= 3,785 milliliters
Quart	= 2 pints		Gallon	= 0.83 Brit. gallon
Quart	= 57.75 cu. in.			
Quart	= 956 milliliters		Liter	= 2.1 pints (liq.)
Quart	= 0.25 gallon		Liter	= 1.06 quarts (liq.)
Quart	= 0.94 liter		Liter	= 1,000 cu. cm.

CAPACITY MEASURE DRY:

Peck	= 0.25 bushel		Bushel	= 2 pecks
Peck	= 16 pints		Bushel	= 64 pints
Peck	= 8 cups		Bushel	= 32 quarts
Peck	= 32 cups		Bushel	= 128 cups

TABLES OF VOLUMES, WEIGHTS AND MEASURES

LINEAR MEASURE:

12 inches	=	1 foot
3 feet	=	1 yard
5 1/2 yards, or 16 1/2 feet	=	1 rod
40 rods	=	1 furlong
8 furlongs, or 320 rods	=	1 mile
1 fathom (marine measure)	=	6 feet (used in measuring depths at sea)
1 knot	=	1.152 mi. (nautical or geographical mi.)
1 league	=	3 knots (3 x 1.15 miles)

CIRCULAR OR ANGULAR MEASURE:

60 seconds	=	1 minute
60 minutes	=	1 degree
360 degrees	=	1 circle
30 degrees	=	1 sign (1/12th of a circle)
60 degrees	=	1 sextant (1/6th of a circle)
90 degrees	=	1 quadrant (1/4th of a circle)

A 90° angle is a right angle.

SQUARE MEASURE:

Square foot	=	144 square inches
Square foot	=	0.111 square yard
Square yard	=	1,296 square inches
Square yard	=	9 square feet
Square rod	=	30 1/4 square yards
Square mile	=	640 acres
Acre	=	43,560 square feet
Acre	=	4,840 square yards
Acre	=	160 square rods

MISCELLANEOUS INFORMATION

One inch of rainfall means 100 tons of water on every acre.

To find the capacity of cylindrical tanks, square the diameter in inches, multiply by the height in inches, and this product by the decimal .34. Point off four decimals, and you have the capacity in gallons.

To find the diameter of a circle, multiply the circumference by .31831.

To find the circumference of a circle, multiply the diameter by 3.1416.

To find the area of a circle, multiply the square of the diameter by .7854.

To find the surface of a ball, multiply the square of the diameter by 3.1416.

To find the side of an equal square, multiply the diameter by .8862.

To find the cubic inches in a ball, multiply the cube of the diameter by .5236.

Doubling the diameter of a pipe increases its capacity four times.

A gallon of water (U.S. Standard) weighs 8½ pounds and contains 231 cubic inches.

A cubic foot of water contains 7½ gallons, 1,728 cubic inches, and weighs 62½ pounds.

Four inches equals 1 hand in measuring horses.

1 link equals 7.92 inches.

1 rod equals 25 links, 16½ feet.

1 mile equals 80 chains, 5280 feet.

TABLE OF DIAMETERS, CIRCUMFERENCES, AND AREAS OF CIRCLES

Diameter	Circumference	Area	Diameter	Circumference	Area
1/8	.3927	.01227	6 1/8	19.242	29.464
1/4	.7854	.04909	6 1/4	19.635	30.679
3/8	1.1781	.1104	6 3/8	20.027	31.919
1/2	1.5708	.1963	6 1/2	20.420	33.183
5/8	1.9635	.3068	6 5/8	20.813	34.471
3/4	2.3562	.4417	6 3/4	21.205	35.784
7/8	2.7489	.6013	6 7/8	21.598	37.122
1	3.1416	.7854	7	21.991	38.484
1 1/8	3.5343	.9940	7 1/8	22.383	39.871
1 1/4	3.9270	1.2271	7 1/4	22.776	41.282
1 3/8	4.3197	1.4848	7 3/8	23.169	42.718
1 1/2	4.7124	1.7671	7 1/2	23.562	44.178
1 5/8	5.1051	2.0739	7 5/8	23.954	45.663
1 3/4	5.4978	2.4052	7 3/4	24.347	47.173
1 7/8	5.8905	2.7611	7 7/8	24.740	48.707
2	6.2832	3.1416	8	25.132	50.265
2 1/8	6.6759	3.5465	8 1/8	25.515	51.848
2 1/4	7.0686	3.9760	8 1/4	25.918	53.456
2 3/8	7.4613	4.4302	8 3/8	26.310	55.088
2 1/2	7.8540	4.9087	8 1/2	26.703	56.745
2 5/8	8.2467	5.4119	8 5/8	27.096	58.426
2 3/4	8.6394	5.9395	8 3/4	27.489	60.132
2 7/8	9.0321	6.4918	8 7/8	27.881	61.862
3	9.4248	7.0686	9	28.274	63.617
3 1/8	9.8175	7.6699	9 1/8	28.667	65.396
3 1/4	10.210	8.2957	9 1/4	29.059	67.200
3 3/8	10.602	8.9462	9 3/8	29.452	69.029
3 1/2	10.995	9.6211	9 1/2	29.845	70.882
3 5/8	11.388	10.320	9 5/8	30.237	72.759
3 3/4	11.781	11.044	9 3/4	30.630	74.662
3 7/8	12.173	11.793	9 7/8	31.023	76.588
4	12.566	12.566	10	31.416	78.540
4 1/8	12.959	13.364	10 1/8	31.808	80.515
4 1/4	13.351	14.186	10 1/4	32.201	82.516
4 3/8	13.744	15.033	10 3/8	32.594	84.540
4 1/2	14.137	15.904	10 1/2	32.986	86.590
4 5/8	14.529	16.800	10 5/8	33.379	88.664
4 3/4	14.922	17.720	10 3/4	33.772	90.762
4 7/8	15.315	18.665	10 7/8	34.164	92.885
5	15.708	19.635	11	34.557	95.033
5 1/8	16.100	20.629	11 1/8	34.950	97.205
5 1/4	16.493	21.647	11 1/4	35.343	99.402
5 3/8	16.886	22.690	11 3/8	35.735	101.623
5 1/2	17.278	23.758	11 1/2	36.128	103.869
5 5/8	17.671	24.850	11 5/8	36.521	106.139
5 3/4	18.064	25.967	11 3/4	36.913	108.434
5 7/8	18.457	27.108	11 7/8	37.306	110.753
6	18.849	28.274	12	37.699	113.097

Diameter	Circumference	Area	Diameter	Circumference	Area
12 1/8	38.091	115.466	18 1/8	56.941	258.016
12 1/4	38.484	117.859	18 1/4	57.334	261.587
12 3/8	38.877	120.276	18 3/8	57.726	265.182
12 1/2	39.270	122.718	18 1/2	58.119	268.803
12 5/8	39.662	125.184	18 5/8	58.512	272.447
12 3/4	40.055	127.676	18 3/4	58.905	276.117
12 7/8	40.448	130.192	18 7/8	59.297	279.811
13	40.840	132.732	19	59.690	283.529
13 1/8	41.233	135.297	19 1/8	60.083	287.272
13 1/4	41.626	137.886	19 1/4	60.475	291.039
13 3/8	42.018	140.500	19 3/8	60.868	294.831
13 1/2	42.411	143.139	19 1/2	61.261	298.648
13 5/8	42.804	145.802	19 5/8	61.653	302.489
13 3/4	43.197	148.489	19 3/4	62.046	306.355
13 7/8	43.589	151.201	19 7/8	62.439	310.245
14	43.982	153.938	20	62.832	314.160
14 1/8	44.375	156.699	20 1/8	63.224	318.099
14 1/4	44.767	159.485	20 1/4	63.617	322.063
14 3/8	45.160	162.295	20 3/8	64.010	326.051
14 1/2	45.553	165.130	20 1/2	64.402	330.064
14 5/8	45.945	167.989	20 5/8	64.795	334.101
14 3/4	46.338	170.873	20 3/4	65.188	338.163
14 7/8	46.731	173.782	20 7/8	65.580	342.250
15	47.124	176.715	21	65.973	346.361
15 1/8	47.516	179.672	21 1/8	66.366	350.497
15 1/4	47.909	182.654	21 1/4	66.759	354.657
15 3/8	48.302	185.661	21 3/8	67.151	358.841
15 1/2	48.694	188.692	21 1/2	67.544	363.051
15 5/8	49.087	191.748	21 5/8	67.937	367.284
15 3/4	49.480	194.828	21 3/4	68.329	371.543
15 7/8	49.872	197.933	21 7/8	68.722	375.826
16	50.265	201.062	22	69.115	380.133
16 1/8	50.658	204.216	22 1/8	69.507	384.465
16 1/4	51.051	207.394	22 1/4	69.900	388.822
16 3/8	51.443	210.597	22 3/8	70.293	393.203
16 1/2	51.836	213.825	22 1/2	70.686	397.608
16 5/8	52.229	217.077	22 5/8	71.078	402.038
16 3/4	52.621	220.353	22 3/4	71.471	406.493
16 7/8	53.014	223.654	22 7/8	71.864	410.972
17	53.407	226.980	23	72.256	415.476
17 1/8	53.799	230.330	23 1/8	72.649	420.004
17 1/4	54.192	233.705	23 1/4	73.042	424.557
17 3/8	54.585	237.104	23 3/8	73.434	429.135
17 1/2	54.978	240.528	23 1/2	73.827	433.731
17 5/8	55.370	243.977	23 5/8	74.220	438.363
17 3/4	55.763	247.450	23 3/4	74.613	443.014
17 7/8	56.156	250.947	23 7/8	75.005	447.699
18	56.548	254.469	24	75.398	452.390

DECIMAL EQUIVALENT TABLE

Decimal	Fractional Equivalent	Decimal	Fractional Equivalent
.01562	1/64	.51562	33/64
.03125	1/32	.53125	17/32
.04687	3/64	.54687	35/64
.0625	1/16	.5625	9/16
.07812	5/64	.57812	37/64
.09375	3/32	.59375	19/32
.10937	7/64	.60937	39/64
.1250	1/8	.6250	5/8
.14062	9/64	.64062	41/64
.15625	5/32	.65625	21/32
.17187	11/64	.67187	43/64
.1785	3/16	.6875	11/16
.20312	13/64	.70312	45/64
.21875	7/32	.71875	23/32
.23437	15/64	.73437	47/64
.2500	1/4	.7500	3/4
.26562	17/64	.76562	49/64
.28125	9/32	.78125	25/32
.29687	19/64	.79687	51/64
.3125	5/16	.8125	13/16
.32812	21/64	.82812	53/64
.34375	11/32	.84375	27/32
.35937	23/64	.85937	55/64
.3750	3/8	.8750	7/8
.39062	25/64	.89062	57/64
.40625	13/32	.90625	29/32
.42187	27/64	.92187	59/64
.4375	7/16	.9375	15/16
.45312	29/64	.95312	61/64
.46875	15/32	.96875	31/32
.48437	31/64	.98437	63/64
.5000	1/2	1.00000	1

SLOPE MEASUREMENT: PLAN (HORIZONTAL) TO TRUE MEASURE

Slope Ratio: Horizontal to Vertical	Map Measure	Multiplied by Factor		True Measure
¾ to 1	x	1.667	=	
1 to 1	x	1.4142	=	
1½ to 1	x	1.2019	=	
2 to 1	x	1.1180	=	
2½ to 1	x	1.0770	=	
3 to 1	x	1.0541	=	
4 to 1	x	1.0198	=	

ANGLES OF SLOPES

Angles (In Degrees and Minutes)	Slope Ratio Equivalent
18 - 25	3:1
26 - 35	2:1
33 - 42	1.5:1
45 - 00	1:1
53 - 00	.75:1
56 - 20	.67:1
63 - 30	.5:1

UNITS OF MEASUREMENT

UNITS OF LIQUID MEASURE—EQUIVALENCES

Gallons	Pounds	Cubic Feet
0.12	1.00	0.016
1.00	8.33	0.134
7.48	62.30	1.00
26.00	216.67	3.48
26.50	220.83	3.54
27.00	225.00	3.61
27.50	229.17	3.68
28.00	233.33	3.75
28.50	237.50	3.81
29.00	241.67	3.88
29.50	245.83	3.95
30.00	250.00	4.01
30.50	254.17	4.08
31.00	258.33	4.15
31.50	262.50	4.21
32.00	266.67	4.28
32.50	270.83	4.35
33.00	275.00	4.41
33.50	279.17	4.48
34.00	283.33	4.55
34.50	287.50	4.61
35.00	291.67	4.68
35.50	295.83	4.75
36.00	300.00	4.82
36.50	304.17	4.88
37.00	308.33	4.95
37.50	312.50	5.02
38.00	316.67	5.08
38.50	320.83	5.15
39.00	325.00	5.22
39.50	329.17	5.28
40.00	333.33	5.35

SCALE EQUIVALENTS
Scales 1" = 100' to 1" = 1,000'

Representative Fraction	Feet per Inch	Sq. Feet per Sq. Inch	Acres
1:1200	100	10,000	.2290
1:2400	200	40,000	.9184
1:3600	300	90,000	2.0661
1:4800	400	160,000	3.6736
1:6000	500	250,000	5.7392
1:7200	600	360,000	8.2644
1:12000	1,000	1,000,000	22.9568

SCALE EQUIVALENTS
Scales 1" = 50' to 1" = 10 Miles

Representative Fraction	Inches per Mile	Miles per Inch	Feet per Inch
1:600	105.6	.0095	50
1:1200	52.8	.0189	100
1:2400	26.4	.0379	200
1:3600	17.6	.0568	300
1:4800	13.2	.0758	400
1:6000	10.56	.0947	500
1:7200	8.8	.1136	600
1:12000	5.28	.1894	1,000
1:63360	1.0	1.0000	5,280
1:316800	0.2	5.0000	26,400
1:633600	0.1	10.0000	52,800

Scale	Feet per Inch	Sq. Feet per Sq. Inch
1/16″ = 1′	16.0	256.0
1/8 ″ = 1′	8.0	64.0
3/8 ″ = 1′	5.33	28.4
1/4 ″ = 1′	4.0	16.0
5/16″ = 1′	3.2	10.24
3/8 ″ = 1′	2.67	7.13
7/16″ = 1′	2.3	5.29
1/2 ″ = 1′	2.0	4.0
9/16″ = 1′	1.77	3.13
5/8 ″ = 1′	1.6	2.56
11/16″ = 1′	1.45	2.1
3/4 ″ = 1′	1.33	1.77
13/16″ = 1′	1.23	1.51
7/8 ″ = 1′	1.14	1.3
15/16″ = 1′	1.06	1.12
1 ″ = 1′	1.0	1.0

SCALE EQUIVALENTS
Scales 1" = 10' to 1" = 80'

Scale	Feet per Inch	Sq. Feet per Inch	Acres
1″ = 10′	10	100	.0023
1″ = 20′	20	400	.0092
1″ = 30′	30	900	.0207
1″ = 40′	40	1,600	.0367
1″ = 50′	50	2,500	.0574
1″ = 60′	60	3,600	.0826
1″ = 66′	66	4,356	.1000
1″ = 70′	70	4,900	.1124
1″ = 80′	80	6,400	.1470

A DECIMAL TABLE OF HOURS

Number of Minutes	Decimal Parts of an Hour	Number of Minutes	Decimal Parts of an Hour
1	.0167	15	.25
2	.0333	20	.333
3	.05	25	.4167
4	.0687	30	.50
5	.0833	35	.5833
6	.10	40	.6667
7	.1168	45	.75
8	.1333	50	.8333
9	.15	55	.9167
10	.1667	60	1.0

RULES FOR COMPUTING INTEREST
360 Day Basis

The following will be found to be excellent rules for finding the interest on any principal for any number of days. When the principal contains cents, point off four places from the right of the results to express the interest in dollars and cents. When the principal contains dollars only, point off two places.

Four Per Cent. — Multiply the principal by the number of days to run, and divide by 90.

Five Per Cent. — Multiply by number of days, and divide by 72.

Six Per Cent. — Multiply by number of days, and divide by 60.

Eight Per Cent. — Multiply by number of days, and divide by 45.

Nine Per Cent. — Multiply by number of days, and divide by 40.

Ten Per Cent. — Multiply by number of days, and divide by 36.

IRREGULAR FIGURE

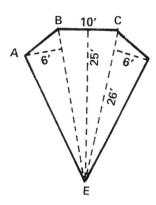

To find area take Triangle B, C, E and add Triangles A, B, E and C, D, E

Example: Triangle B, C, E, 5 x 25 = 125 sq. ft.
  ''   A, B, E 13 x 6 = 78 sq. ft.
  ''   C. D. E 13 x 6 — 78 sq. ft.
                               281 sq. ft.

TRAPESIUM

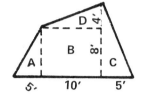

To find the area of this figure take the area of Square B and add the areas of the three Triangles A, C and D.

Example: Square B   10 x 8   = 80
           Triangle A   8 x 2½ = 20
           ''   C   12 x 2½ = 30
           ''   D   5 x 4 = 20
                      Total   150 sq. ft.

HEXAGON

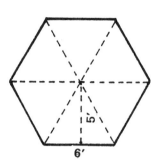

To find area multiply six times the area of one triangle.
Example: 6 x 3 x 5 = 90 sq. ft.

OCTAGON

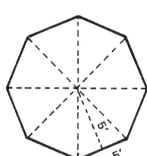

To find the area multiply eight times the area of one triangle.
Example: 8 x 6 x 2 = 216 sq. ft.

PENTAGON

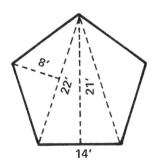

To find the area take the area of Triangle A and add the areas of Triangles B & C.

Example: Triangle A   7 x 21 = 147 sq. ft.
          ''   B 11 x 8 = 88 '' ''
          ''   C 11 x 8 = 88 '' ''

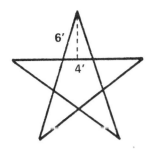

FIVE POINT STAR

To find area multiply 8 times the area of one triangle.
Example: 6 x 2 x 8 = 96 sq. ft.

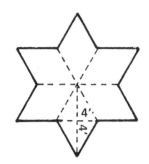

SIX POINT STAR

To find area multiply 12 times the area of one triangle.
Example: 4 x 2 x 12 = 96 sq. ft.

DIAMOND

To find the area multiply twice the area of one triangle.
Example: 18 x 6 x 2 = 216 sq. ft.

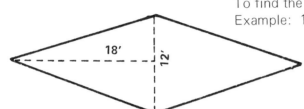

CRESCENT

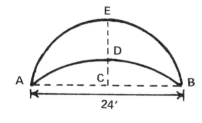

To find the area of a crescent connect points A & B. This base forms diameter of complete circle. Figure the area of the complete circle and divide the result by 4.
Example: 24 x 24 x .7854 = 452 sq. ft.
            452 divided by 4 = 113 sq. ft.

Note: The point D is half the distance between the points C and E. Should the crescent be narrower, deduct 17½% off the area for each foot of the line from point D to point E. Similarly, if the Crescent is wider, add 17½% for each foot of the line from point D to point C.

SEGMENT OF CIRCLE

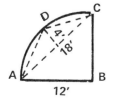

To find area, take area of Triangle A, B, and C and add Triangle A, D, and C and add 10%.
Example: Triangle A, B, C = 6 x 12 = 72
                A, D, C = 9 x 4 = 36
                                   ―――
                                   108
                                    11
                                   ―――
                                   119 sq. ft.

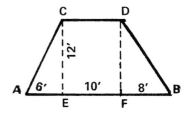

IRREGULAR FIGURE

To find area take area of Oblong C, D, E and F, add Triangles
A. C, E and B, D, F

Example: Oblong C, D, E, F,   10 x 12 = 120 sq. ft.
       Triangle A, C, E   12 x 3 = 36 '' ''
         ''   B, D, F   12 x 4 = 48 '' ''
                              204 '' ''

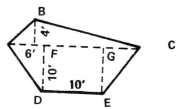

IRREGULAR FIGURE

To find area take square D, E, F, G and add triangles A, D, F;
D, E, G and A, B, C.

Example: Square E, E, F, G = 10 x 10 = 100 sq. ft.
       Triangle   A, D, F = 10 x 3 = 30 '' ''
         ''   C, E, G = 10 x 3 = 30 '' ''
         ''   A, B, C = 11 x 4 = 38 '' ''
                               198 '' ''

CIRCLE

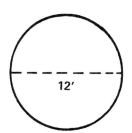

To find the circumference of a circle, multiply diameter by 3.1416.
Example: 12 x 3.1416 = 37.7 linear ft.

To find the area of a Circle, square the diameter and multiply by .7854.
Example: 12 x 12 x .7854 = 113.1 sq. ft.

ELLIPSE

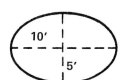

To find the area of an Ellipse, multiply diameters by each other and multiply by .7854.
Example: 10 x 5 x .7854 = 39.3 sq. ft.

SQUARE/RECTANGLE

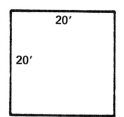
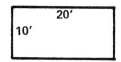

To find the area of a square or rectangle, multiply height by width.
Example:

Square 20' x 10' = 400 sq. ft.
Oblong 20' x 10' = 400 sq. ft.

TRIANGLES

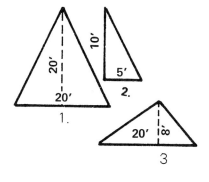
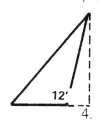

To find the area of any Triangle, take half the base and multiply by the height.
Examples:

1. 10 x 20   = 200 sq. ft.
2. 10 x 2½ = 25 sq. ft.
3. 10 x 8   = 80 sq. ft.
4.   6 x 18   = 108 sq. ft.

PARALLELOGRAM

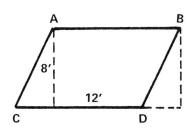

To find the area of this figure, form the square A, B, C, D and multiply base by height.
Example: 12 x 8 = 96 sq. ft.

SIMPLE INTEREST TABLE

	Time	4%	5%	6%	7%	8%	10%	12%	14%	16%
$ 1.00	1 month	$.003	$.004	$.005	$.005	$.006	.008	.010	.011	.013
"	2 months	.007	.008	.010	.011	.013	.016	.020	.023	.026
"	3 "	.010	.013	.015	.017	.020	.026	.030	.034	.040
"	6 "	.020	.025	.030	.035	.040	.050	.060	.070	.080
"	12 "	.040	.050	.060	.070	.080	.100	.120	.140	.160
$100.00	1 day	.011	.013	.016	.019	.022	.026	.032	.030	.044
"	2 days	.022	.027	.032	.038	.044	.054	.064	.076	.088
"	3 "	.034	.041	.050	.058	.067	.082	.100	.116	.134
$100.00	4 days	$.045	$.053	$.066	$.077	$.089	.106	.132	.154	.178
"	5 "	.056	.069	.082	.097	.111	.138	.164	.194	.222
"	6 "	.067	.083	.100	.116	.133	.166	.200	.232	.266
"	1 month	.334	.416	.500	.583	.667	.832	1.000	1.166	1.334
"	2 months	.667	.832	1.000	1.166	1.333	1.664	2.000	2.332	2.666
"	3 "	1.000	1.250	1.500	1.750	2.000	2.500	3.000	3.500	4.000
"	6 "	2.000	2.500	3.000	3.500	4.000	5.000	6.000	7.000	8.000
"	12 "	4.000	5.000	6.000	7.000	8.000	10.000	12.000	14.000	16.000

INTEREST
CHARGES FOR 30 DAYS

Balance Due on Principal	5%	6%	7%	8%	10%	12%	14%	16%
$ 1	.00	.01	.01	.01	.02	.02	.02	.02
2	.01	.01	.01	.01	.02	.02	.03	.03
3	.01	.02	.02	.02	.02	.04	.04	.05
4	.02	.02	.02	.03	.04	.04	.05	.06
5	.02	.03	.03	.03	.04	.06	.06	.07
6	.03	.03	.04	.04	.06	.06	.08	.09
7	.03	.04	.04	.05	.06	.08	.09	.10
8	.03	.04	.05	.05	.06	.08	.09	.11
9	.04	.05	.05	.06	.08	.10	.11	.13
10	.04	.05	.06	.07	.08	.10	.12	.14
20	.08	.10	.12	.13	.16	.20	.24	.26
30	.13	.15	.18	.20	.26	.30	.36	.40
40	.17	.20	.23	.27	.34	.40	.46	.54
50	.21	.25	.29	.33	.42	.50	.58	.66
60	.25	.30	.35	.40	.50	.60	.70	.80
70	.29	.35	.41	.47	.58	.70	.82	.94
80	.33	.40	.47	.53	.66	.80	.94	1.06
90	.38	.45	.53	.60	.76	.90	1.06	1.20
$ 100	.42	.50	.58	.67	.84	1.00	1.08	1.34
200	.83	1.00	1.17	1.33	1.66	2.00	2.34	2.66
300	1.25	1.50	1.75	2.00	2.50	3.00	3.50	4.00
400	1.67	2.00	2.33	2.67	3.34	4.00	4.66	5.34
500	2.08	2.50	2.92	3.33	4.16	5.00	5.84	6.66
600	2.50	3.00	3.50	4.00	5.00	6.00	7.00	8.00
700	2.92	3.50	4.08	4.67	5.84	7.00	8.16	9.34
800	3.33	4.00	4.67	5.33	6.66	8.00	9.34	10.66
900	3.75	4.50	5.25	6.00	7.50	9.00	10.50	12.00
1,000	4.17	5.00	5.38	6.67	8.34	10.00	11.66	13.34
2,000	8.33	10.00	11.67	13.33	16.66	20.00	23.34	26.66
3,000	12.50	15.00	17.50	20.00	25.00	30.00	35.00	40.00
4,000	16.67	20.00	23.33	26.67	33.34	40.00	46.66	53.34
5,000	20.83	25.00	29.17	33.33	41.66	50.00	58.34	66.66
6,000	25.00	30.00	35.00	40.00	50.00	60.00	70.00	80.00
7,000	29.17	35.00	40.83	46.67	58.34	70.00	81.66	93.34
8,000	33.33	40.00	46.67	53.33	66.66	80.00	93.34	106.66
9,000	37.50	45.00	52.50	60.00	75.00	90.00	105.00	120.00

FUNGICIDE TOXICITY
By Dr. C. C. Powell, The Ohio State University

Acute Oral and Skin Toxicity of Fungicides. Fungicides are generally not considered dangerous. However, they are pesticides and **do** have toxic properties. Furthermore, the toxic properties of any pesticide can be intensified with other exposure factors. A compound with very low acute toxicity can indeed be hazardous if large amounts are used, if it is volatile, if it is handled carelessly, or if it is used constantly over a season by any particular person. For any pesticide there will be individuals who will be unusually sensitive or allergic to the chemicals. Furthermore, there are pesticide hazards classed as chronic or low level, long term. These are not always related to acute hazards! Be careful when using **any** pesticide!

LD_{50} values refer to the dose in milligrams of chemical per kilogram of body weight that proves to be lethal to 50% of a test population of adult rats. We know this test to be a fairly good measure of relative acute danger to humans. It depends on body weight—the bigger the body, the harder you are to kill! The lower the LD_{50} value, the greater the toxicity. When you look over the following table, remember that aspirin, a material considered slightly toxic, has an LD_{50} value of 1,200 mg/kg. Deaths from misuse or accidental use of aspirin are far greater per year than deaths from pesticides.

This table is appropriate for a 180-pound man.

Chemical	Oral LD_{50}	Lethal Dose		Skin Reaction*
Actidione (100% pure)	2	0.0056	oz.	Severe
Benlate	9,590	18.8	oz.	Mild
Captan	9,000-15,000	27-30	oz	Mild
Copper	3,000-6,000	9	oz.	Mild
Daconil 2787	3,750	11	oz.	Mild
Dexom	60	.17	oz.	Mild
Difolatan	5,600-6,200	-13.8	oz.	Severe
Maneb	6,750-	20.2	oz.	Moderate
Mancozek (FORE)	8,000	24	oz.	Mild
Terraclor (PCNB)	1,200-2,000	3.6	oz.	Moderate
Terrazole (Truban)	2,000	6.0	oz.	?
Thiram	780	2.3	oz.	Severe
Zineb	5,200	15.6	oz.	Moderate

*Skin reaction potential

Weighing out pesticides is the best and most accurate way to achieve the correct dose. It is easy to weigh out the chemicals if we are making up 100 gallons of spray. Commercial applicators should **always** weigh materials! However, home applicators and others dealing with small jobs may need only a gallon or so of spray. A kitchen scale or other "cheapy" is not too accurate when dealing in 1/10 ounce measures. For these measures, accuracy is probably improved by measuring **level** teaspoons (not packed down). The following list is accurate to the nearest ¼ teaspoon. Even though you may use this table as a guide, **please be sure and read all labels to make certain you are using the product legally.**

Product	Rate/100 Gals.	Tsps*/Gal.
Agri-strep 21.5 WP	½ lb.	1
Benlate (Tersan 1991) 50 WP	½ lb.	1¼
Basic Copper Sulphate (Tribasic)	4 lbs.	4½
Copper sulphate (Pentahydrate)	4 lbs.	3½
Daconil 2787 75 WP	1½ lbs.	2¾
Dyrene 50 WP	1 lb.	1½
Flotox 90 WP	4 lbs.	4½
Fore 80 WP	1½ lbs.	2½
Karathane (Mildex) 25 WP	½ lb.	¾
Maneb 80 WP	1½ lbs.	2½
Orthocide (Captan) 50 WP	2 lbs.	3
Phaltan (Folpet) 75 WP	1½ lbs.	2½
Thiram 65 WP	1½ lbs.	2¼
Zineb 75 WP	1½ lbs.	3

*Sometimes, chemical companies change formulations that may throw the densities off. Always check labels for the latest information.

ADDITIONS TO COST PRICE NECESSARY TO ACHIEVE SPECIFIC GROSS PROFIT

Cost Price	Plus	Equals	Gross Profit
x	100%		50%
x	66-2/3%		40%
x	53-4/5%		35%
x	42-6/7%		30%
x	33-1/3%		25%
x	25%		20%
x	17-2/3%		15%
x	14-2/7%		12½%
x	11-1/9%		10%
x	8-2/3%		8%
x	5-1/4%		5%

UNITS OF MEASUREMENT

CONVERSION FACTORS

INCHES IN DECIMALS OF A FOOT

1/16	.0052	1	.0833
8/82	.0078	2	.1667
1/8	.0104	3	.2500
8/16	.0156	4	.3333
1/4	.0208	5	.4167
5/16	.0260	6	.5000
8/8	.0313	7	.5833
1/2	.0417	8	.6667
5/8	.0521	9	.7500
3/4	.0625	10	.8333
7/8	.0729	11	.9167

EQUIVALENTS OF CAPACITY

(All measures are level full)

3 teaspoons	1 tablespoon
1/2 fluid ounce	1 tablespoon
16 tablespoons	1 cup
2 gills	1 cup
1/2 liquid pint	1 cup
8 fluid ounces	1 cup
1 liquid pint	2 cups
16 fluid ounces	2 cups

DRY MEASURE

2 pints---------------------1 quart	4 pecks------------------1 bushel
8 quarts--------------------1 peck	36 bushels---------------1 chaldron

MEASUREMENT OF TIME–CONVERSIONS
Minutes to Decimal Hours

Min. = Hrs.	Min. = Hrs.	Min. = Hrs.	Min. = Hrs.
1 = .017	16 = .267	31 = .517	46 = .767
2 = .034	17 = .284	32 = .534	47 = .784
3 = .050	18 = .300	33 = .550	48 = .800
4 = .067	19 = .317	34 = .567	49 = .817
5 = .084	20 = .334	35 = .584	50 = .834
6 = .100	21 = .350	36 = .600	51 = .850
7 = .117	22 = .368	37 = .617	52 = .867
8 = .135	23 = .384	38 = .634	53 = .884
9 = .150	24 = .400	39 = .650	54 = .900
10 = .167	25 = .417	40 = .667	55 = .917
11 = .184	26 = .434	41 = .684	56 = .934
12 = .200	27 = .450	42 = .700	57 = .950
13 = .217	28 = .467	43 = .717	58 = .967
14 = .232	29 = .484	44 = .734	59 = .984
15 = .250	30 = .500	45 = .750	60 = 1.000

MEASUREMENT OF TIME

60 Seconds.	1 Minute
60 Minutes.	1 Hours
24 Hours	1 Day
7 Days	1 Week
52 Weeks	1 Year
366 Days.	1 Leap Year
360 Days.	1 Commercial Year
10 Years	1 Decade
100 Years	1 Century

To convert	Multiply by
Cubic inches to cubic centimeters	16·39
Cubic feet to cubic metres	0·028
Cubic yards to cubic metres	0·764
Cubic Metres to cubic feet	35·315
Cubic metres to cubic yards	1·308
U.K. pints to U.S. liquid pints	1·201
U.K. gallons to U.S. gallons	1·201
U.K. pints to litres	0·568
U.K. gallons to litres	4·546
U.S. liquid pints to U.K. pints	0·568
U.S. gallons to U.K. gallons	0·833
U.S. liquid pints to U.K. pints	0·833
U.S. liquid pints to litres	0·473
U.S. gallons to litres	3·785

NOTE

An Imperial Bushel is a dry measure equivalent to 8 U.K. gallons or 4 pecks, and contains 1·28 cubic feet (e.g. 10 in x 10 in x 22 in)

	Cubic metres	Litres	U.S. liquid pints	U.S. gallons
1 cubic foot	0·028	28·316	59·844	7·480
1 cubic yard	0·764	764·5	—	—
1 U.K. pint	—	0·568	1·201	0·150
1 U.K. gallon	0·0045	4·546	9·607	1·201

	Cubic feet	Cubic yards	U.K. pints	U.K. gallons
1 cubic metre	35·315	1·308	—	—
1 litre	0·035	—	1·760	0·220
1 U.S. liquid pint	0·017	—	0·833	0·104
1 U.S. gallon	0·134	—	6·661	0·833

UNITS OF WEIGHT		CONVERSIONS
Unit	Multiplied By	Equals
Grains	.002286	Ounces
Ounces	.0625	Pounds
Ounces	.00003125	Tons
Pounds	16.00	Ounces
Pounds	0.01	Hundredweight
Pounds	.0005	Tons
Tons	32000.00	Ounces
Tons	2000.00	Pounds

UNITS OF VOLUME:		CONVERSIONS
Unit	Multiplied By	Equals
Cubic Inches	.0005787	Cubic Feet
Cubic Inches	.0000214	Cubic Yards
Cubic Inches	.0043	U. S. Gallons
Cubic Feet	1728.00	Cubic Inches
Cubic Feet	.03704	Cubic Yards
Cubic Feet	7.48	U. S. Gallons
Cubic Yards	46656.00	Cubic Inches
Cubic Yards	27.00	Cubic Feet
Cubic Yards	202.00	U. S. Gallons

DRY MATERIALS:
CONVERSIONS FOR USE FOR SMALL AREAS

Rate/Acre (in Lbs.)	Rate/1,000 Sq. Ft. (in Ounces)	Rate/100 Sq Ft
1 pound(s)	.35 ounce(s)	.25 teaspoon(s)
2 "	.7 "	.50 "
3 "	1.1 "	.75 "
4 "	1.4 "	1.00 "
5 "	1.8 "	1.25 "
6 "	2.1 "	1.50 "
8 "	2.8 "	1.75 "
10 "	3.7 "	2.00 "
20 "	7.3 "	0.73 ounces
40 "	14.0 "	1.40 "
50 "	18.0 "	1.80 "
100 "	37.0 "	3.70 "
200 "	73.0 "	7.30 "
300 "	110.0 "	11.00 "
400 "	147.0 "	14.70 "
500 "	184.0 ..	18.40 "

TO CHANGE CUBIC FEET TO GALLONS:

Multiply the number of cubic feet by 7.48. For approximate results, multiply by 7 1/2.

TO CHANGE GALLONS TO CUBIC FEET:

Multiply the number of gallons by 0.1337.

TO CHANGE CUBIC INCHES TO GALLONS:

Divide the number of cubic inches by 231, or multiply by 0.004329.

TO CHANGE CUBIC FEET TO BUSHELS:

Divide the number of cubic feet by 1.244. For approximate results, multiply the number of cubic feet by 4/5.

TO CHANGE CUBIC INCHES TO BUSHELS:

Divide the number of cubic inches by 2.50.42 or multiply the number of cubic inches by 0.000465.

TO CHANGE BUSHELS TO CUBIC FEET:

Multiply the number of bushels by 1.244. For approximate results, multiply the number of bushels by 5/4.

TO CHANGE TEMPERATURE IN DEGREES CENTIGRADE TO DEGREES FAHRENHEIT:

Multiply Centigrade temperature by 9/5 and add 32°.
Example: 30°C. = 30 x 9/5 + 32 = 86°F.

TO CHANGE TEMPERATURE IN DEGREES FAHRENHEIT TO DEGREES CENTIGRADE:

Subtract 32 from Fahrenheit reading and multiply by 5/9.
Example: 86°F. = 86 - 32 = 54 x 5/9 = 30°C.

CONVERSION FACTORS

To change cubic feet to gallons.
Multiply the number of cubic feet by 7.48. For approximate results multiply by 7½.

To change gallons to cubic feet.
Multiply the number of gallons by 0.1337.

To change cubic inches to gallons.
Divide the number of cubic inches by 231, or multiply by 0.004329.

To change cubic feet to bushels.
Divide the number of cubic feet by 1.244. For approximate results multiply the number of cubic feet by 4/5.

To change cubic inches to bushels.
Divide the number of cubic inches by 2150.42, or multiply the number of cubic inches by 0.000465.

To change bushels to cubic feet.
Multiply the number of bushels by 1.244. For approximate results multiply the number of bushels by 5/4.

CONVERSION TABLES (U.S.)

Linear Measure

1 foot = 12 inches
1 yard = 3 feet
1 rod = 5.5 yards = 16.5 feet
1 mile = 160 rods = 1760 yards = 5280 feet

Square Measure

1 square foot (sq. ft.) = 144 square inches (sq. inch)
1 square yard (sq. yd.) = 9 sq. feet
1 square rod (sq. rd.) = 272.25 sq. ft. = 30.25 sq. yd.
1 acre—43560 sq. ft. = 4840 sq. yds. = 160 sq. rds.
1 square mile = 640 acres

Liquid Capacity Measure

1 tablespoon = 3 teaspoons
1 fluid ounce = 2 tablespoons
1 cup = 8 fluid ounces
1 pint = 2 cups = 16 fluid ounces
1 quart = 2 pints = 32 fluid ounces
1 gallon = 4 quarts = 8 pints = 128 fluid ounces

Cubic Measure

1 cubic foot (cu. ft.) = 1728 cubic inches (cu. in.) = 29.922
liquid quarts = 7.48 gallons
1 cubic yard = 27 cubic feet

Weight Measure

1 pound (lb.) = 16 ounces
1 hundred weight (cwt.) = 100 pounds
1 ton = 20 cwt. = 2000 pounds

Rates of Application

1 ounce/sq. ft. = 2722.5 lbs./acre
1 ounce/sq. yd. = 302.5 lbs./acre
1 ounce/100 sq. ft. = 27.2 lbs./acre
1 pound/100 sq. ft. = 435.6 lbs./acre
1 pound/1000 sq. ft. = 43.6 lbs./acre
1 gallon/acre = 1/3 ounce/1000 sq. ft.
5 gallons/acre = 1 pint/1000 sq. ft.
100 gallons/acre = 2.5 gallons/1000 sq. ft. = 1 quart/100 sq. ft.
100 lbs./acre = 2.5 lbs./1000 sq. ft.

Test Plot Conversion Table

1 kilogram (kg) = 1000 grams (g) = 2.2 lbs.
1 gram (g) = 1000 milligrams (mg) = .35 ounce
1 liter = 1000 milliliters (ml)
  or cubic centimeters (cc) = 1.058 quarts
1 milliliter or cubic centimeter = .034 fluid ounce
1 milliliter or cubic centimeter of water weighs 1gram
1 liter of water weighs 1 kilogram
1 lb. = 435.6 grams
1 ounce = 28.35 grams
1 pt. of water weighs approximately 1 lb.
1 gallon of water weighs approximately 8.34 lbs.

1 gallon = 4 qts. = 3.785 liters
1 qt. = 2 pts. = 9.46 liters
1 pt. = .473 liters
1 fluid ounce = 29.6 milliliters or cubic centimeters

1 part per million (PPM) = 1 milligram/liter
                         = 1 milligram/kilogram
                         = .0001 per cent
                         = .013 ounces by in 100 gallons of water

1 percent = 10,000 ppm
               = 10 grams per liter
               = 10 grams per kilogram
               = 1.33 ounces by weight per gallon of water
               = 8.34 pounds/100 gallons of water

.1 percent = 1000 ppm = 1000 milligrams/liter
.01 percent = 100 ppm = 100 milligrams/liter
.001 percent = 10 ppm = 10 milligrams/liter
.0001 percent = 1 ppm = 1 milligram/liter

CONVERSION TABLES (U.S.)

Width of Area Covered to Acres Per Mile Traveled

Width of Strip (feet)	Acres/mile
6	.72
10	1.21
12	1.45
16	1.93
18	2.18
20	2.42
25	3.02
30	3.63
50	6.04
75	9.06
100	12.1
150	18.14
200	24.2
300	36.3

CONVERSION TABLES (U.S.)

Miles Per Hour Converted to Feet Per Minute

MPH	fpm
1	88
2	176
3	264
4	352

CONVERSION TABLES (U.S.)

Useful Measurements

Length

1 mile = 80 chains = 8 furlongs = 1760 yards = 5280 ft. =
  1.6 kilometres
1 chain = 22 yards = 4 rods, poles or perches = 100 links

Weight

1 long ton = 20 cwt = 2240 lbs.
1 lb. = 16 ozs. = 454 grams = 0.454 kilograms
1 short ton = 2000 lbs.
1 metric ton = 2204 lbs. = 1000 kilograms

Area

1 acre = 10 sq. chains = 4840 sq. yards = 43560 sq. ft. =
  0.405 hectares
1 sq. mile = 640 acres = 2.59 kilometres
1 hectare = 2.471 acres

Volume

1 gallon = 4 quarts = 8 pints = 160 fluid ozs. =
  1.2 U.S. gallons = 4.546 litres
1 fluid oz. = 2 tablespoons = 4 dessertspoons =
  8 teaspoons = 28.4 c.c.'s
1 litre = 1000 c.c.'s = 0.22 gallons = 1.76 pints

Capacities

Cylinder — diameter^2/ x depth x 0.785 = cubic feet
Rectangle — breadth x depth x length = cubic feet
Cubic Feet x 6.25 = gallons

Quick Conversions

1 pint/acre	= 1 fluid oz./242 sq. yards
1 gal./acre	= 1 pint/605 sq. yards
1 lb./acre	= 1 oz./300 sq. yards
1 cwt./acre	= 0.37 oz./sq. yard
1 m.p.h.	= 88 ft./minute
3 m.p.h.	= 1 chain/15 sec.
1 litre/hectare	= 0.089 gal./acre
1 kilogram/hectare	= 0.892 lb./acre
1 c.c./100 litres	= 0.16 fl. oz./100 gallons
125 c.c./100 litres	= 1 pint/100 gallons
1 gm./100 litres	= 0.16 oz./100 gallons

A strip 3 ft. wide x 220 chains)
A strip 4 ft. wide x 165 chains)   1 acre
A strip 5 ft. wide x 132 chains)

MEASUREMENT OF TIME—CONVERSIONS
Miles Per Hour to Feet Per Minute

Miles per Hour*	Feet per Minute	Time Needed to Travel Various Distances Expressed in Seconds				
		100 Feet	200 Feet	300 Feet	400 Feet	500 Feet
1	88	68.0	137.0	205.0	272.0	340.0
2	176	34.0	68.0	102.0	136.0	170.0
3	264	23.0	46.0	69.0	92.0	115.0
4	352	17.0	34.0	51.0	68.0	85.0
5	440	13.6	27.0	41.0	54.4	68.0
6	528	11.3	22.6	34.0	45.2	56.5
7	618	9.7	19.4	29.0	38.8	48.5
8	704	8.5	17.0	27.0	34.0	42.5
10	880	6.8	13.6	20.4	27.2	34.0
20	1,760	3.4	6.8	10.2	13.6	17.0
30	2,640	2.3	4.6	6.9	9.2	11.5
40	3,520	1.7	3.4	5.1	6.8	8.5
50	4,400	1.4	2.8	4.2	5.6	7.0
60	5,280	1.1	2.2	3.3	4.4	5.5

*One Mile per Hour = 88 Feet per Minute = 1.467 Feet per Second.

TEMPERATURE CONVERSION

Fahrenheidt to Centigrade	Centigrade to Fahrenheidt
Degrees F. to Degrees C.	Degrees C. to Degrees F.
−40 = −40.0	−40 = −40
−30 = −34.4	−30 = −22
−20 = −28.9	−20 = −4
−10 = −23.3	−10 = +14
0 = −17.8	0 = +32
+10 = −12.2	+10 = +50
+20 = −6.67	+20 = +68
+32 = −0.00	+30 = +86
+50 = +10.0	+50 = +122
+60 = +15.6	+60 = +140
+80 = +26.7	+80 = +176
+100 = +37.8	+100 = +212
+212 = +100.0	

Centigrade = (F. − 32 degrees) x 5/9   Fahrenheidt = (C. x 9/5 + 32 degrees)

MEASUREMENT OF LENGTH—CONVERSIONS

English Feet	=	Metric Meters	Metric Meters	=	English Feet
1	=	.3048	1	=	3.2808
2	=	.6096	2	=	6.5616
3	=	.9144	3	=	9.8425
4	=	1.2192	4	=	13.1233
5	=	1.5240	5	=	16.4041
6	=	1.8288	6	=	19.6850
7	=	2.1336	7	=	22.9658
8	=	2.4384	8	=	26.2466
9	=	2.7432	9	=	29.5275
10	=	3.0480	10	=	32.8083

MEASUREMENT OF LENGTH—CONVERSIONS

English Statute Miles	=	Metric Kilometers	Metric Kilometers	=	English Statute Miles
1	=	1.6093	1	=	.62137
2	=	3.2186	2	=	1.24274
3	=	4.8279	3	=	1.86411
4	=	6.4372	4	=	2.48548
5	=	8.0465	5	=	3.10685
6	=	9.6558	6	=	3.72822
7	=	11.2651	7	=	4.34959
8	=	12.8744	8	=	4.97096
9	=	14.4837	9	=	5.59233
10	=	16.0930	10	=	6.21370

CONVERSION FACTORS

MEASUREMENT OF LENGTH–CONVERSIONS

English Inches	=	Metric Centimeters	Metric Centimeters	=	English Inches
1	=	2.54	1	=	.3937
2	=	5.08	2	=	.7874
3	=	7.62	3	=	1.1811
4	=	10.16	4	=	1.5748
5	=	12.70	5	=	1.9685
6	=	15.24	6	=	2.3622
7	=	17.78	7	=	2.7559
8	=	20.32	8	=	3.1496
9	=	22.86	9	=	3.5433
10	=	25.40	10	=	3.9370

MEASUREMENT OF LENGTH–CONVERSIONS
Inches and Fractions to Decimal Parts of a Foot

	Fractions Of An Inch							
	0	1/8	1/4	3/8	1/2	5/8	3/4	7/8
0″	.000	.010	.021	.031	.042	.052	.063	.073
1″	.083	.094	.104	.115	.125	.135	.146	.156
2″	.167	.177	.188	.198	.208	.219	.229	.240
3″	.250	.260	.271	.281	.292	.302	.313	.323
4″	.333	.344	.354	.365	.375	.385	.396	.406
5″	.417	.427	.438	.448	.458	.469	.479	.490
6″	.500	.510	.521	.531	.542	.552	.563	.573
7″	.583	.594	.604	.615	.625	.635	.646	.656
8″	.667	.677	.688	.698	.708	.719	.729	.740
9″	.750	.760	.771	.781	.792	.802	.813	.823
10″	.833	.844	.854	.865	.875	.885	.896	.906
11″	.918	.927	.938	.948	.958	.969	.979	.990

Example: 6 1/2″ = .542 foot

To use chart: Find the point where the full inch wanted in the left column intersects with the fraction wanted in its column.

MEASUREMENT OF VOLUME—CONVERSIONS
English System to Metric System

Unit		Multiplied By		Equals
Cubic Inches	x	16.40	=	Cubic Centimeters
Cubic Feet	x	0.0283	=	Cubic Meters
Cubic Yards	x	0.765	=	Cubic Meters

MEASUREMENT OF VOLUME—CONVERSIONS
Metric System to English System

Unit		Multiplied By		Equals
Cubic Centimeters	x	.06	=	Cubic Inches
Cubic Meters	x	35.3	=	Cubic Feet
Cubic Meters	x	1.31	=	Cubic Yards

PLACE VALUES IN DECIMAL SYSTEM

hundred-thousandths	ten-thousandths	thousandths	hundredths	tenths	decimal point	units	tens	hundreds	thousands	ten thousands	hundred thousands	millions
+	+	+	+	+	+	+	+	+	+	+	+	+

UNITS OF LIQUID MEASURE: WEIGHT EQUIVALENTS

1 Pint	16 Ounces
1 Quart	32 Ounces
1 Gallon	128 Ounces
1 Teaspoon	.167 Ounces
1 Tablespoon	.5 Ounces

LIQUID MATERIALS: CONVERSIONS FOR USE FOR SMALL AREAS

Rate/Acre	Rate/1,000 Sq. Ft.	Rate/100 Sq. Ft.
1 pint	0.36 fl. oz.	0.25 teaspoons
1 quart	0.72 " "	0.50 "
1 gallon	2.90 " "	2.00 "
2 "	5.90 " "	4.00 "
3 "	8.80 " "	2.00 tablespoons
5 "	14.70 " "	3.00 "
10 "	29.40 " "	6.00 "
15 "	2.80 pints	9.00 "
20 "	3.70 "	12.00 "
25 "	2.30 quarts	15.00 "
50 "	4.60 "	1.84 cups
75 "	6.90 "	2.76 "
100 "	9.19 "	3.67 "
200 "	18.37 "	7.35 "

AREA CONVERSION:
ACRES TO EQUIVALENT SQUARE FOOTAGE

ACRE As Fraction	ACRE As Decimal	EQUIVALENT SQUARE FOOTAGE
1/1000	.001	43.56
1/100	.01	435.60
1/10	.1	4,356.00
1/8	.125	5,445.00
1/4	.250	10,890.00
1/3	.333	14,520.00
1/2	.500	21,780.00
3/4	.750	32,670.00
1/1	1.000	43,560.00
1-1/8	1.125	49,005.00
1-1/4	1.250	54,450.00
1-1/3	1.333	58,080.00
1-1/2	1.500	65,340.00
1-3/4	1.750	76,230.00
2	2.000	87,120.00
2-1/2	2.500	108,900.00
3	3.000	130,680.00
3-1/2	3.500	152,460.00
4	4.000	174,240.00
4-1/2	4.500	196,020.00
5	5.000	217,800.00

AREA CONVERSION—ACRES TO EQUIVALENT SQUARE FOOTAGE

Acre As Fraction	Acre As Decimal	Equivalent Square Footage
1/1000	.001	43.56
1/100	.01	435.60
1/10	.10	4,356.00
1/8	.125	5,445.00
1/4	.250	10,890.00
1/3	.333	14,520.00
1/2	.500	21,780.00
3/4	.750	32,670.00
1/1	1.000	43,560.00
1 1/8	1.125	49,005.00
1 1/4	1.250	54,450.00
1 1/3	1.333	58,080.00
1 1/2	1.500	65,340.00
1 3/4	1.750	76,230.00
2	2.000	87,120.00
2 1/2	2.500	108,900.00
3	3.000	130,680.00
3 1/2	3.500	152,460.00
4	4.000	174,240.00
4 1/2	4.500	196,020.00
5	5.000	217,800.00

AREA CONVERSION—SQUARE FEET TO EQUIVALENT ACREAGE

Square Feet	Acres	Square Feet	Acres
1,000	.0230	41,000	.9412
2,000	.0459	42,000	.9642
3,000	.0689	43,000	.9871
4,000	.0918	43,560	1.0000
5,000	.1148	65,340	1.5000
6,000	.1377	87,120	2.0000
7,000	.1607	108,900	2.5000
8,000	.1837	130,680	3.0000
9,000	.2066	152,460	3.5000
10,000	.2296	174,240	4.0000
11,000	.2525	196,020	4.5000
12,000	.2755	217,800	5.0000
13,000	.2984	239,580	5.5000
14,000	.3214	261,360	6.0000
15,000	.3444	283,140	6.5000
16,000	.3673	304,920	7.0000
17,000	.3903	326,700	7.5000
18,000	.4132	348,480	8.0000
19,000	.4362	370,260	8.5000
20,000	.4591	392,040	9.0000
21,000	.4821	413,820	9.5000
22,000	.5051	435,600	10.0000
23,000	.5280	871,200	20.0000
24,000	.5510	1,089,000	30.0000
25,000	.5739	1,742,400	40.0000
26,000	.5969	2,178,000	50.0000
27,000	.6198	2,613,600	60.0000
28,000	.6428	3,049,200	70.0000
29,000	.6657	3,484,800	80.0000
30,000	.6887	3,920,400	90.0000
31,000	.7117	4,356,000	100.0000
32,000	.7346	8,712,000	200.0000
33,000	.7576	10,890,000	300.0000
34,000	.7805	17,424,000	400.0000
35,000	.8035	21,780,000	500.0000
36,000	.8264	26,136,000	600.0000
37,000	.8494	30,492,000	700.0000
38,000	.8724	34,848,000	800.0000
39,000	.8953	39,204,000	900.0000
40,000	.9183	43,560,000	1,000.0000

UNITS OF LENGTH—CONVERSIONS

Unit	Multiplied By	Equals
Inches	0.0833	Feet
Inches	0.02778	Yards
Inches	0.0050	Rods
Inches	0.0000158	Miles
Feet	0.333	Yards
Feet	0.0606	Rods
Feet	0.0001894	Miles
Yards	36.00	Inches
Yards	3.00	Feet
Yards	0.0005681	Miles
Miles	63,360.00	Inches
Miles	5,280.00	Feet
Miles	1,760.00	Yards
Miles	320.00	Rods
Miles	80.00	Chains

UNITS OF AREA—CONVERSIONS

Unit	Multiplied By	Equals
Square Inches	.007	Square Feet
Square Inches	.00077	Square Yards
Square Feet	144.00	Square Inches
Square Feet	.11111	Square Yards
Square Yards	1,296.00	Square Inches
Square Yards	9.00	Square Feet
Square Yards	.033	Square Rods
Square Rods	.00625	Acres
Square Miles	640.00	Acres

CONVERSION FACTORS

UNITS OF LIQUID MEASURE: CONVERSIONS

Units	Multiplied By:	Equals
Gills	.5	Cups
Gills	7.23	Cubic Inches
Gills	0.2500	Pints
Gills	0.1250	Quarts
Gills	0.03125	Gallons
Cups	2.00	Gills
Cups	0.5	Pints
Pints	4.0	Gills
Pints	2.0	Cups
Pints	0.5	Quarts
Pints	0.1250	Gallons
Quarts	2.0	Pints
Quarts	0.250	Gallons
Gallons	4.0	Quarts
Gallons	8.0	Pints
Gallons	231.0	Cubic Inches

DRY MATERIALS—CONVERSIONS FOR USE IN SMALL AREAS

Rate per Acre in Pounds	Rate per 1,000 Sq. Ft. in Ounces	Rate per 100 Sq. Ft.
1	.35	.25 teaspoons
2	.7	.50 "
3	1.1	.75 "
4	1.4	1.00 "
5	1.8	1.25 "
6	2.1	1.50 "
8	2.8	1.75 "
10	3.7	2.00 "
20	7.3	0.73 ounces
40	14.0	1.40 "
50	18.0	1.80 "
100	37.0	3.70 "
200	73.0	7.30 "
300	110.0	11.00 "
400	147.0	14.70 "
500	184.0	18.40 "

UNITS OF LIQUID MEASURE—WEIGHT EQUIVALENTS

Unit	Equals	
1 Pint	16.0	Ounces
1 Quart	32.0	Ounces
1 Gallon	128.0	Ounces
1 Teaspoon	0.167	Ounces
1 Tablespoon	0.5	Ounces

UNITS OF DRY MEASURE: CONVERSIONS

Units	Multiplied By	Equals
Pints	0.5	Quarts
Pints	33.6	Cubic Inches
Pints	0.0625	Pecks
Pints	0.01562	Bushels
Quarts	2.0	Pints
Quarts	0.1250	Pecks
Quarts	0.03125	Bushels
Pecks	16.0	Pints
Pecks	8.0	Quarts
Pecks	0.2500	Bushels
Bushels	4.0	Pecks
Bushels	32.0	Quarts
Bushels	64.0	Pints
Bushels	2,150.4	Cubic Inches

WEIGHT: CONVERSION FACTORS

To Convert	Multiply By
Hundredweights to kilograms	50.8
Hundredweights to tons	0.051
Hundredweights to U.S. short hundredweights	1.12
Hundredweights to U.S. short tons	0.056
Tons to kilograms	1,016.0
Tons to tonnes	1.016
Tons to U.S. short hundredweights	22.4
Tons to U.S. short tons	1.12
Tonnes to hundredweights	19.684
Tonnes to tons	0.984
Tonnes to U.S. short hundredweights	22.046
Tonnes to U.S. short tons	1.102
U.S. short hundredweights to hundredweights	0.893
U.S. short hundredweights to tons	0.045
U.S. short hundredweights to kilograms	45.359
U.S. short hundredweights to tons	0.045
U.S. short tons to hundredweights	17.857
U.S. short tons to tons	0.893
U.S. short tons to kilograms	907.185
U.S. short tons to tonnes	0.907

AREA: CONVERSION FACTORS

To Convert	Multiply By
Square feet to square meters	0.093
Square yards to square meters	0.836
Acres to hectares	0.405
Square miles to hectares	258.9
Square meters to square feet	10.76
Square meters to square yards	1.196
Hectares to acres	2.471
Hectares to square miles	0.0039

Note: 1. An acre is equivalent to a square of 208' 8" side. A hectare is equivalent to a square of 100 miles side.
2. Irish, Scottish and Welsh acres may occasionally be encountered. They vary in different parts of the British Isles from 3.240 square yards to 9,780 square yards.

WEIGHT: CONVERSION TABLES

	Kilogram	Ton	U.S. Short Hundredweight	U.S. Short Ton
1 pound	0.45	0.00045	0.01	0.0005
1 hundredweight	50.8	0.0508	1.12	0.056
1 ton	1,016.0	1.016	22.4	1.12

	Pound	Hundredweight	Ton
1 ton	2,204.62	19.684	0.984
1 kilogram	2.205	0.020	-
1 U.S. short hundredweight	100.0	0.893	0.045
1 U.S. short ton	2,000.0	17.857	0.893

WEIGHT: CONVERSION FACTORS

To Convert	Multiply By
Ounces per square yard to grams per square mile	33.906
Ounces per square yard to kilograms per hectare	339.057
Pounds per acre to grams per square mile	0.112
Pounds per acre to kilograms per hectare	1.121
Grams per square mile to ounces per square yard	0.029
Grams per square mile to pounds per acre	8.922
Kilograms per hectare to ounces per square yard	0.003
Kilograms per hectare to pounds per acre	0.892

AREA: CONVERSION FACTORS

To Convert	Multiply By
Meters to Inches	39.37
Meters to feet	3.280
Meters to yards	1.093
Kilometers to miles	0.6214
Inches to meters	0.025
Feet to meters	0.304
Yards to meters	0.914
Miles to kilometers	1.609

LINEAR MEASURE: CONVERSION TABLES

	Centimeters	Meters	Kilometers
1 inch	2.54	0.025	0.00002
1 foot	30.48	0.304	0.00030
1 yard	91.44	0.914	0.00091
1 mile	-	1,609.344	1.60934

	Inch	Foot	Yard
1 centimeter	0.303	0.032	0.010
1 meter	39.370	3.280	1.093
1 kilometer	-	3,280.8	1,093.6

CONVERSION FACTORS

To convert	Multiply by
Metres to inches	39.37
Metres to feet	3.280
Metres to yards	1.093
Kilometres to miles	0.6214
Inches to metres	0.025
Feet to metres	0.304
Yards to metres	0.914
Miles to kilometres	1.609

CONVERSION FACTORS

To convert	Multiply by
Square feet to square metres	0.093
Square yards to square metres	0.836
Acres to hectares	0.405
Square miles to hectares	258.9
Square metres to square feet	10.76
Square metres to square yards	1.196
Hectares to acres	2.471
Hectares to square miles	0.0039

Note:

An acre is equivalent to a square of 208 ft. 8 in. side. A hectare is equivalent to a square of 100 m. side.

THICKNESS PER SQUARE YARD TO CUBIC YARDS PER ACRE

Inch thickness per square yard	Cubic yards per acre	Inch thickness per square yard	Cubic yards per acre
½	67*	3¾*	500
¾*	100	4	538*
1	134-1/2*	6	806-2/3
1½*	200	7½*	1000
2	269*	12	1613-1/3
2¼*	300	24	3226-2/3
3	403-1/3	36	4840

*approximate

WEIGHT PER UNIT AREA

Ounces per square yard	Pounds per acre	Hundredweights per acre	Tons per acre
3/8*	112	1	
1/2	151¼	1-1/3*	
3/4	224	2	
1	302½	2-2/3*	
1-1/2*	448	4	
1-3/4*	560	5	¼
2	605	5-1/2*	
2-1/4*	672	6	
3*	896	8	
3¾*	1,120	10	½
4	1,210	10¾*	
7½*	2,240	20	1
15*	4,480	40	2
29*	8,960	80	4
60*	17,920	160	8
74*	22,400	200	10

*approximate

WORKABLE CONVERSIONS FOR SOIL AREAS

1 oz. per sq. ft. equals 2,722.5 lbs. per acre

1 oz. per sq. yard equals 302.5 lbs. per acre.

I oz. per 100 sq. ft. equals 27.2 lbs. per acre.

1 lb. per 100 sq. ft. equals 435.6 lbs. per acre.

1 lb. per 1,000 sq. ft. equals 43.6 lbs. per acre.

1 lb. per acre equals 1/3 oz. per 1,000 sq. ft.

5 gals. per acre equals 1 pint per 1,000 sq. ft.

100 gals. per acre equals 2.5 gals. per 1,000 sq. ft.

100 gals. per acre equals 1 quart per 100 sq. ft.

100 gals. per acre equals 2.5 lbs. per 1,000 ft.

WEIGHTS AND COVERAGES OF MATERIALS

Top Soil:

6 wheelbarrow loads equal one cubic yard
1 cubic yard loose weighs 2,000 lbs.
1 cubic yard compacted weighs 2,400 lbs.
1 cubic yard loose will cover

324 sq. ft. 1" deep	36 sq. ft. 9" deep
162 sq. ft. 2" deep	32 sq. ft. 10" deep
108 sq. ft. 3" deep	27 sq. ft. 12" deep
81 sq. ft. 4" deep	21 sq. ft. 15" deep
54 sq. ft. 6" deep	18 sq. ft. 18" deep
40 sq. ft. 8" deep	13 sq. ft. 24" deep

One acre requiring topsoil 6" deep will take 807 cu. yds. loose.
Add 20% for compacting.

Peat Moss:

1 Bale contains 20 to 22 Bushels compacted. When broken up and loosened, one bale
will cover

240 sq. ft. 1" deep
120 sq. ft. 2" deep
80 sq. ft. 3" deep

One acre of ground requiring a mulch of 2" Peat Moss will take 363 Bales.

Manure:
(rotted)

1 cubic yard average weight 800 lbs.

Humus:

1 cubic yard average weight 1,050 lbs.
To figure quantities use same as Topsoil

WORKABLE CONVERSIONS FOR SOIL AREAS

1 oz. per sq. ft.	=	2,722.5 lbs. per acre
1 oz. per sq. yard	=	302.5 lbs. per acre
1 oz. per 100 sq. ft.	=	27.2 lbs. per acre
1 lb. per 100 sq. ft.	=	435.6 lbs. per acre
1 lb. per 1,000 sq. ft.	=	43.6 lbs. per acre
1 lbs. per acre	=	1/3 oz. per 1,000 sq. ft.
5 gals. per acre	=	1 pt. per 1,000 sq. ft.
100 gals. per acre	=	2.5 gals. per 1,000 sq. ft.
100 gals. per acre	=	1 qt. per 100 sq. ft.
100 gals. per acre	=	2.5 lbs. per 1,000 sq. ft.

DILUTION CHART

TO GET A SOLUTION	ADD PER GALLON WATER	
	OZ.	CONCENTRATE MEASURE
5 to 1	24	3 Cups
10 to 1	12	1½ Cups
15 to 1	8	1 Cup
20 to 1	6	¾ Cup
30 to 1	4	½ Cup
40 to 1	3	6 Tbsp.
60 to 1	2	4 Tbsp.
80 to 1	1½	3 Tbsp.
100 to 1	1¼	2½ Tbsp.

CONVERSION FACTORS

UNITS OF AREA		CONVERSIONS
Units	Multiplied By	Equals
Square Inches	.007	Square Feet
Square Inches	.00077	Square Yards
Square Feet	144.0	Square Inches
Square Feet	.11111	Square Yards
Square Yards	1296.00	Square Inches
Square Yards	9.00	Square Feet
Square Yards	.033	Square Rods
Square Rods	.00625	Acres
Square Miles	640.00	Acres

Ounces per square yard	Pounds per acre	Hundredweights per acre	Tons per acre
3*	896	8	
3¾*	1,120	10	½
4	1,210	10¾*	
7½*	2,240	20	1
15*	4,480	40	2
29*	8,960	80	4
60*	17,920	160	8
74*	22,400	200	10

METRIC CONVERSIONS

LENGTH

Imperial		Metric	Metric		Imperial
1 inch	=	2.540 centimetres	1 centimetre	=	0.3937 inch
1 foot	=	0.3048 metre	1 decimetre	=	0.3281 foot
1 yard	=	0.9144 metre	1 metre	=	3.281 feet 1.094 yards
1 rod	=	5.029 metres	1 decametre	=	10.94 yards
1 mile	=	1.609 kilometres	1 kilometre	=	0.6214 mile

WEIGHT

Imperial		Metric	Metric		Imperial
1 ounce (troy)	=	31.103 grams	1 gram	=	0.032 oz. (troy)
1 ounce (avoir.)	=	28.350 grams	1 gram	=	0.035 oz. (avoir.)
1 lb. (troy)	=	373.242 grams	1 kilogram	=	2.679 lbs. (troy)
1 lb. (avoir.)	=	453.592 grams	1 kilogram	=	2.205 lbs. (avoir.)
1 ton (short)	=	0.907 ton*	1 ton	=	1.102 tons (short)

*1 ton equals 1,000 kilograms.

VOLUME

Imperial		Metric	Metric		Imperial
1 quart	=	1.137 litres	1 litre	=	0.880 quart
1 gallon	=	4.546 litres	1 litre	=	0.220 gallon
1 bushel	=	35.238 litres	1 hectolitre	=	2.838 bushels
1 cubic inch	=	16.393 cu. centimetres	1 cu. centimetre	=	0.061 cubic inch
1 cubic foot	=	28.571 cu. decimetres	1 cu. decimetre	=	0.035 cubic foot
1 cubic yard	=	0.765 cubic metre	1 cubic metre	=	1.308 cubic yards

AREA

Imperial		Metric	Metric		Imperial
1 sq. inch	=	6.452 sq. centimetres	1 sq. centimetre	=	0.155 sq. inch
1 sq. foot	=	0.093 sq. metre	1 sq. metre	=	10.76 sq. feet
1 sq. yard	=	0.836 sq. metre	1 sq. metre	=	1.196 sq. yards
1 acre	=	0.405 hectare*	1 hectare	=	2.471 acres
1 sq. mile	=	259.1 hectares	1 sq. kilometre	=	0.386 sq. mile
1 sq. mile	=	2.590 kilometres			

*1 hectare is synonymous with a "square hectometre".

HOW TO ESTIMATE LANDSCAPE COSTS
BIBLIOGRAPHY
(in order of date of publication)

Surtees, John

Landscaping Master Units —Series 1

A Ready Reckoner for Estimating Quantities of Top Soil, Manure, Humus, Fertilizers, Etc., Excavation Tree Pits, Tree Balls, Hedges, Lawns, Areas, Weights, Designs, Truck and Car Lots.
John Surtees, Cost Analyst,   Ridgefield, Conn.
(out-of-print)

Surtees, John

First Section of Landscaping Costs — Series 2

A Text Book Covering Costs of Landscaping, Digging, Delivery, Planting, Lawns, Overhead, Maintenance, Guarantees, Any Job, Any Size, Anywhere.
John Surtees, Cost Analyst   Ridgefield, Conn.
(out of print)

Surtees, John

Second Section — Continuation of Series 2 — Series 3

Covering More Costs of Landscaping, Large Tree Moving, Removing Existing Trees, Cemetery Plantings, Street Tree Plantings, Basic Erosion, Hedges, Drainage, Unloading Cars, Soils, Organic Matter, Waste, Plans, Labor Report Forms.
John Surtee, Cost Analyst   Ridgefield, Conn.
(out-of-print)

Surtees, John

Nursery Cost Finding

A Textbook for the use of Nurserymen, Growers of Fruit Trees, Perennials. Landscape Designers. A Manual of Cost Finding Covering Cost of Production, Maintenance, and all Other Operations, Labor Charts — Working Graphs, Examples.
Published by Walter De La Mare Co., Inc.
New York City
(out-of-print)

Basic Building Data

1949. Van Nostrand-Reinhold Publishing Company, Litton Educational Publishing, 7625 Empire Drive, Florence, Kentucky 41042.

228

Robinette, Gary O.

Off The Board/Into The Ground

Techniques of Planting Design Implementation, William C. Brown Book Co., Dubuque, Iowa, 1968. 367 pp.

Architectural Graphic Standards

6th ed., 1970. John Wiley & Sons, Inc., 1 Wiley Drive, Somerset, New Jersey 08873.

National Crushed Stone Association

Design Guide for Permanent Parking Areas — Featuring Crushed Stone Base

1972. National Crushed Stone Association, 1415 Elliot Place, NW, Washington, D.C. 20007.

Griffin, James M.

Landscape Data Manual

Building News, Inc. 3055 Overland Ave., Los Angeles, California, 90034, Copyright California Landscape Contractors Association, 6252 Telegraph Road, Los Angeles, California 190040.
(Second Printing 1972) 160 pp.

American Association of Nurserymen, Inc.

The American Standard for Nursery Stock

Z 60.1, 1973. American Association of Nurserymen, Inc., 230 Southern Building, Washington, D.C. 20005.

Time Saver Standards — A Handbook of Architectural Designs

5th ed., 1974. McGraw-Hill Book Company, P.O. Box 400, Hightstown, New Jersey 08520.

National Crushed Stone Association

Design Guide for Streets — Featuring Crushed Stone Base

1975. National Crushed Stone Association, 1415 Elliot Place, NW, Washington, D.C. 20007.

Cooperative Extension Service University of Maryland

Guideline Specification — Soil Preparation and Sodding

Md—Va. Publication No. 1, 1976. Cooperative Extension Service, University of Maryland, College Park, Maryland 20742.

Nelson, William R.,Jr.

Landscaping Your Home

Circular 1111, August, 1977. Agricultural Publications Office, 123 Mumford Hall, University of Illinois, Urbana, Illinois 61801.

National Landscape Association

Landscape Designers and Estimators Guide (Revised Edition)

National Landscape Association, 230 Southern Building, Washington, D. C. 20005. Copyright 1978, 60 pp.

Landphair, Harlow C. and Fred Klatt,Jr.

Landscape Architecture Construction

Elsivier North Holland, Inc. 52 Vanderbilt Ave., New York, N.Y. , 10017, 1979, 432 pp.

Packard, Robert T. (Editor)

Architectural Graphic Standards

John Wiley & Sons, New York, N.Y. 1981, 785 pp.

Kerr, Kathleen W.

Cost Data for Landscape Construction

Kerr Associates, Inc. 1942 Irving Avenue, South, Minneapolis, Minnesota 55403, 1982, (Annual update).

Means, Robert Snow

Building Construction Cost Data

(Annual update)   Robert Snow Means Company, Inc. 100 Construction Plaza, Kingston, Ma. 08634, 1982, 406 pp.

Kerr, Kathleen W. (Editor)

L.A. FILE, The Landscape Architecture Catalog File

Landscape Architecture Magazine, 1190 East Broadway, Louisville, Ky. 40204, 1982, unpaged.

Pereira, Percival E.

Dodge Construction Systems Costs

McGraw-Hill's Cost Information Systems, McGraw-Hill Information Co., 1221 Avenue of the Americas, New York, N.Y. 10020.